CYPRESS TREE ODYSSEY

D1329912

Making Sense of Trials & Tests
On & Off the Golf Course

TODD R. DUFEK

NEW YORK

CYPRESS TREE ODYSSEY
By Todd R. Dufek
© 2008 Todd R. Dufek. All rights reserved.

ISBN: 978-1-60037-328-2   **Paperback**

Published by:

MORGAN · JAMES
THE ENTREPRENEURIAL PUBLISHER™
Morgan James Publishing, LLC
1225 Franklin Ave Ste 325
Garden City, NY 11530-1693
Toll Free 800-485-4943
www.MorganJamesPublishing.com

Habitat
for Humanity®
Peninsula
Building Partner

Cover and Interior Design by:
Heather Kirk
www.GraphicsByHeather.com
Heather@GraphicsByHeather.com

Cover Photography, "*Point Lobos 2161*" & "*Left Coast Sunset*" By:
Hugh F. Pierson
h. Ford Pierson Photography LLC
14 Aliso Road
Carmel Valley, CA 93924
www.hFordPierson.com

Library of Congress Control Number: 2007935676

DEDICATION

To my wife Michelle and my sweet daughter Beth—
thank you for allowing me the time I needed to complete
this book. I love you both and am blessed beyond words
to have you in my life.

IV

Mike –
It was a great thrill to watch you win the masters and take on Tiger and beat him in your backyard in the President's Cup. Now that I admire how you've handled yourself in the spotlight and lived for Christ. I hope you enjoy the book and that it will minister to you.

ACKNOWLEDGMENTS

I can give only one acknowledgment, and that is to my Lord and Savior Jesus Christ. Christ is the reason I survived the grief and losses I experienced, and He is the one who gave me this book as a gift to share with others.

In Christ,
Todd Dufek
John 16:33

email: tmdufek@cox.net

VI

TABLE OF CONTENTS

PREFACE

I t was through the writing of this book that I realized that I simultaneously came to Christ and was bitten hard by the "golf bug" at age 14. Of course, from that day in October of 1972, the day I accepted Christ, I pledged to put Him first in my life. But to be honest, the game of golf sat on the throne much of the time. And I pretty much defined my self-worth by how well I played the game.

Two Junior Club Championships, two High School State Team Championships, a District Team Championship and being named to the first NAIA Academic-All American Golf Team in college, among other honors, left me feeling pretty good about myself. But God knew my heart and my view of life was in for a drastic change.

Through a series of losses and trials, God showed me that golf was merely a game, the importance of material things was vanity, and the only thing of any real value was my relationship with Jesus Christ. Someone could have sat me down and told me those things a hundred times during the years in question. But until I lived through the tests that drove those points home, none of it would have made any sense.

Now when I tee it up, I carry my clubs and Christ carries me through every round of golf and life. I hope that as you read this book you will find that it mirrors the notion that God loves each of us more than we can possibly imagine. And that He is always in control despite our deepest doubts.

Keep your head down and hit it long and straight!

FOREWORD

We are conceived in the dark and born into the light, destined to live in a mixture of both. Yet if we know the Creator through acceptance of Jesus Christ as Lord, we can walk in the light no matter the height of our joy or the depth of our emotional or situational blackness.

This book, **CYPRESS TREE ODYSSEY:** *Making Sense of Trials and Tests On and Off the Golf Course*, combines the uniqueness of an allegory set on the Monterey Peninsula with thoughts on the Christian walk and the game of golf. As you read this work you will follow the progress of a thoroughly unique pilgrim on its journey to know God, and struggle with it as it overcomes its own dark obstacles on its way to the light.

Along the way you will read truths from God's word and receive encouragement that will give your spiritual life and golf game a lift. And finally, you will see how God is involved in every step you take — on and off the course.

Todd R. Dufek

INTRODUCTION

Books written on golf in decades past have likened it to a journey. As have those works that have come out in recent years that eloquently combine thoughts about the game with timeless Christian principles, such as "In His Grip" by Jim Sheard and Wally Armstrong (Word Publishing, 1997). To say that golf is a journey, that it parallels life, is stating the obvious. What is not so clear is that there are underpinnings to the pursuit that can reach the innermost parts of our souls and connect us more deeply with our Creator.

It has also been said that Christian maturity is not a destination to be reached but a process each of us undergoes as we become more like our Savior. As my dad often said, "If we were perfect we'd be in heaven already."

The same is true in the game of golf. None of us will ever play the game perfectly. Despite what all those people hawking new clubs and gadgets say on countless infomercials on *The Golf Channel.* Yet it is in the process of succeeding or failing to send a small round object in the desired direction that the player is shaped during and between each stroke.

Often in our Christian experience we become prideful and confident that we know what God is up to, what He is doing by allowing specific tests into our lives, and how it will all turn out in the end. Only to discover that what God had in mind was totally different than what we expected.

We too, as golfers, can stand on the first tee certain that all parts of our game are in order, that we are destined for the best round in our lives, only to have "the wheels come off." Instead of having our confidence and pride reinforced in life and in golf, we are taught an important lesson in humility.

Could this be the fate of the pilgrim in this book?

Read on.

BEFORE YOU BEGIN THE JOURNEY

Because this book is unlike anything you've ever read, I wanted to pass on a few thoughts that will make it more understandable, enjoyable and relevant to your walk with Christ. The allegory itself is in normal font. Applicable scripture verses are set apart from the text of the allegory in each chapter by a box and refer to a story element or concepts that precede it.

Separated from the body of the tale, yet sprinkled throughout its text, are a variety of "keys" that lend themselves to prayer, meditation and reflection. They are *italicized* and are termed, **KEY OF ENCOURAGEMENT** and **KEY TO A CONCLUSION**. They too refer to the principle(s) preceding them within the allegory.

The former will embolden you to turn to God for strength and wisdom as you face trials and tests off and on the golf course. The latter asks questions and provides commentary that, along with prayer and the guidance of the Holy Spirit, can allow you to discover how God would have you apply this work to your life.

The final keys — **A Grateful Heart** and **On Course** — are also detached from the text and are in a different font.

While **A Grateful Heart** fosters an attitude of thankfulness for the blessings God has given each one of us in life and through the game. **On Course** provides golf tips from swing mechanics to course management. But more significantly, offers themes shared by Christianity and golf.

It is important to remember that because of the book's unique format it can be read a number of different ways. If you are in a contemplative mood and need a healthy escape from the modern stresses of life, read just the allegory. If besieged by trials and tests, you may want to focus on the scriptures that promise God's presence and help during such times.

If your desire is to be encouraged, seek God's answers to some of life's tougher questions, receive some golf instruction, ponder the common ground shared by golf and Christianity or consider what the Lord has done for you, do so by looking over the keys. Your last option is to read the book holistically, or page by page as written. What you will soon discover is that this symbolic story has a cadence and rhythm all its own.

Finally, whatever approach you take to this work, my sincerest desire and prayer is that if you do not know Christ as your personal Savior that you will ask Him into your heart and life. And that if you have been born again, that God would use the odyssey on the pages ahead to draw you into a deeper relationship with Him.

XVIII

PART 1

Born into Darkness

PART ONE
Born into Darkness

Darkness is wrapped around me like a shroud. I do not know how I came to be; I am but a small part of a seed that lies deep inside the earth's warm, rich soil.

Key Verse — Psalm 139:15

My frame was not hidden from you when I was made in the secret place. When I was woven together in the depths of the earth, your eyes saw my unformed body.

KEY OF ENCOURAGEMENT: *Even though hidden and made in secret, God created each one of us as unique, special and different. Yet even with these differences and our human flaws, He loves us beyond measure.*

3

I can hear a pounding now, thunderous. Moisture reaches the soil that envelops me, and the seed I am a part of is refreshed. Nothing, nothing is as sweet as the water that comes from above. Do I feel movement? There it is again! Is it possible for an all encompassing darkness to grow a shade less black? I think it can! The seed I am locked within has split, and I am rising slowly through the mineral-laden earth toward an unknown goal.

With the passage of time, more rumblings and refreshment, I rise further inside the black, dank mustiness. I learn from the soil that holds me that I am part of a grand design yet to be played out, that from this darkness I will find purpose.

KEY OF ENCOURAGEMENT: *Whether you are just becoming aware of the existence of God or faith in Christ has grown in you for a generation, in times of personal darkness it is difficult to find hope and purpose. Acknowledge Christ as Lord of your life. Ask for wisdom and you will find purpose in your testing both on the golf course and in the course of life.*

KEY TO A CONCLUSION: *His path and purpose for you included the game of golf. What do you think God is trying to teach you through a pursuit that demands perfection, but no matter what level of skill you attain, you will never fully master?*

A Grateful Heart

Maybe it was decades ago or perhaps last week, but someone somewhere took the time to introduce you to Christ and to golf. Take a moment and thank God for the person(s).

6

PART 2

Above the Soil

Part Two
Above the Soil

s I rise through the earth, I hear distant scrapes and cracks. It is the sound of soil and stone being cast aside as large roots dig deeper and deeper. Blackness is all I know, but I feel relief that I am not alone.

Key Verse — Isaiah 41:10
So do not fear, for I am with you; do not be dismayed, for I am your God. I will strengthen you and help you; I will uphold you with my righteous right hand.

KEY TO ENCOURAGEMENT: *Christ loved us before we were born, even before we had a personal relationship with Him. And once we know Him personally, there is noth-*

ing on earth that can keep His love from us. We will never be alone, here or in eternity.

On Course
If we have Christ in our lives we will be loved forever. And a "walk spoiled," as Mark Twain called the game of golf, can become a pilgrimage within His creation.

With the passing of more time I burst forth from the soil. Born from it I rise above a thick bed of decaying leaves. I am bombarded by new sensations: bright golden sunlight, cool fresh salt air, sweet green grasses, and mists that roll across a landscape blanketed in green beneath a bright blue sky.

A Grateful Heart
In the midst of playing a round of golf, we are often guilty of failing to appreciate God's handiwork — the beauty of the grass, trees and surroundings. During your next round, take time to praise Him for the course you walk upon and the golf skills you own.

I bask and warm myself in the sunshine and shiver in the cold and dampness of night when the sun hides behind the emerald sea. I come to know the cycle of dark and light, of the wind and stillness, as I slowly come forth from the side of a small weed-like plant. I would try to communicate, but I am still too far within.

Eventually, I see others about me in focus. The objects that rise from the leaf-strewn ground around me are trees; trees with large trunks grayed by the passing of countless days whose branches are contorted and twisted as they pour from the sides of each massive plant. Rough, weathered, with thin scale-like leaves of effervescent green that form lopsided headdresses, they are a curious mixture of ugliness and beauty.

From the ocean winds that wander by, I learn that these are the rarest and most fantastic of earth's trees, the cypresses. I am part of one of their seedlings. They are part of me; I am part of them. This grove of seven has grown to form a natural wall against the elements, their shape and texture a beautiful response to the forces that have caressed and crashed into them over countless years.

Key Verse: Romans 5:3-5

Not only so, but we also rejoice in our sufferings, because we know that suffering produces perseverance; perseverance, character; and character hope.

KEY TO A CONCLUSION: *Is what we become in life a direct result of what we do with the forces or tests that come* *into our lives? Should we choose to see them as opportunities for growth or circumstances that embitter us and alienate us from God?*

On Course

How you react to double and triple bogeys — and worse — determines what type of golfer you become. Put them behind you and use them as a challenge to do well on the next hole, or let the debacle ruin your round. The choice is yours.

Gray mosses have tangled themselves in the branches of each tree, mosses that collect moisture during misty mornings and give up their sparkling droplets with the brilliant rays of sunlit afternoons. Taken as a group, the cypresses look timeworn and old, yet strong.

They would know much about rising above the grasp of the soil while absorbing its precious food, for they tower high above me.

Key Verse — Hebrews 5:13-14
Anyone who lives on milk, being still an infant, is not acquainted with the teachings about righteousness. But solid food is for the mature, who by constant use have trained themselves to distinguish good from evil.

KEY TO CONCLUSION: *What Believers can you look to for the "spiritual nutrients" you need to walk closely with Christ? Learn from them and grow.*

One day, with a bright summer sun shining down upon them from a cloudless sky, the cypresses gave me this:

> *We are trees of glory*
>
> *that grow along the coast,*
>
> *mirroring our Father,*
>
> *the Giver of all Grace.*
>
> *The roughness of our bark*
>
> *stands for what He did*
>
> *on a cross of wood*
>
> *beneath a blackened sky.*
>
> *Our crown of emerald leaves*
>
> *and sturdy twisted limbs*
>
> *means He paid the ransom*
>
> *for all of mankind.*

Key Verse: Mark 10:45

For even the Son of Man did not come to be served, but to serve, and to give his life as a ransom for many.

A Grateful Heart

Thank Him for what He did for you as you play golf and participate daily in the most challenging sport — the game of life.

I did not know their god, and inquired what they meant by their discussion of the "Father" and the "Giver of all Grace." During the days and nights that fell away unnumbered into the past, I learned about the love of this god as the cypresses around me had. I also realized that deep down inside all creatures had knowledge of a benevolent Creator. Creatures that walked the earth's floor knew of him, as did the birds of the air.

I discovered the latter to be true when one landed on me, a timid rusty-brown limb extending from the young sapling that grew strong from the ground. The winged one was garbed in beige and badger brown feathers. Her ebony eyes sparkled and reflected light more gingerly than ocean waves at midday. Her feet danced over my braided ridges and tickled me as her song rose into a sapphire sky.

> *To your grove I come,*
>
> *from the heavens up on high,*
>
> *to tell you as you grow*
>
> *that He's the master of it all.*

He is nature's beauty and balance,

powerful and majestic,

as He is so described,

as it is given to us.

KEY TO ENCOURAGEMENT: *A swing thought or a tip can come from a variety of places. The important thing is the result, not the source. Ask Jack Nicklaus. He found a solution to a swing problem in a dream and an end to his putting woes by taking a tip from his wife.*

God sends his messengers to share the gospel with us so we can be saved. And often, they are the most unlikely people to bring us this eternal "tip."

The cypress forest joined the bird in a chorus, and I knew the words!

Somehow this god must have placed them deep inside me. Feeling life even more fully, I sang too.

God's love, how glorious,

to simply be within it!

To know He forever cares

about all that He created

fills us with such joy.

His praises we must sing!

For many days and nights, through salt air breezes, banks of ocean mist, cloudless spring days, and blazing sunsets in summertime, the elders continued their praises to God. All the while I grew from my tree. Branches leaped from my widening limb, twigs from branches, deep green leaves from twigs.

Many of the Creator's animals wandered into the grove and from each I heard of His goodness. They came inside days splashed in sunshine with the fragrance of flowers on the wind, and days when gray and sullen fog obscured the ocean.

On Course

The mercy and grace that God extends to us is not limited by our life circumstances or how many over par we are. Ever heard of a so-called "Fair Weather Golfer"? These are players that prefer to play the game only when the weather is pleasant.

Thankfully, we do not serve a "Fair Weather God." No matter how we play on the course or what we encounter in life, God is always with us. He walks by our side like a loyal caddy long in our employ, carrying our "bag" of burdens and encouraging us on every step — on the course or off.

An exhausted fox, having failed to catch a rabbit, rested in my shade one sultry spring day. As she stood beneath me panting, her tongue hanging out the side of her mouth, from her tired eyes I gathered this.

Oh young cypress tree,

I'm thankful for your branch

that spreads upon the ground,

a cool and tranquil shade.

Long has been my run

after my quarry today,

that I rest beneath you

to thank Him for all He gave:

for a coat of red,

for fleetness with my feet,

for healthy playful kits

who are coming to know His name.

Key Verse — Psalm 147:7-9

Sing to the Lord with thanksgiving; make music to our God on the harp. He covers the sky with clouds; He supplies the earth with rain and makes grass grow on the hills.

Give thanks to God for all you have — not just the game.

KEY TO A CONCLUSION: *If God makes the rain to fall and the grass to grow, do we owe Him our gratitude for the golf courses we play on?*

The fox lay down and fell into a sound sleep inside my shadow. The sun rose steadily in the cloudless sky, but I refused to yield my shade to its movement. Instead I strained every fiber of my wood — risked breaking —so that one of His creatures could nap within my coolness.

Key Verse — Psalm 36:7
How priceless is your unfailing love! Both high and low among men find refuge in the shadow of your wings.

KEY OF ENCOURAGEMENT: *Always remember, God extends His grace to us so that we might dwell in His "shadow" and find rest.*

There the red one remained until she awoke and, with newfound strength, bounded happily away.

Key Verse — 1 Thessalonians 5:11

Therefore, encourage one another and build each other up, just as in fact you are doing.

On Course

Most golfers, whether playing for fun or caught up in the fiercest of competitions, encourage each other or acknowledge a good effort with a, "Good Shot" or "Good swing."

It may come as a surprise to learn that touring golf professionals on the LPGA and PGA Tours routinely give each other swing tips. Why? Because by encouraging those they play with and against to get better, they must improve as well. We, at the very least, owe that to each other as Believers — especially off the course.

God's blessed ones visited our grove from inside the sky and on top of the ground as the months passed. Sometimes they shared their knowledge of distant places, but always sang His praises. Each time, I thought deep within myself how it — this place, the ocean — all came to be.

KEY TO A CONCLUSION: *Do we have any reason to doubt or wonder about who created the world, everything in it, and why?*

The oldest of the cypresses, known by everyone as "The Grand One," had seen the sun rise and set more than thirty thousand times. But even he could not explain how a seed locks a tree within itself. Or how each living thing in and near the grove had been given the ability to reproduce itself and survive inside of nature.

KEY OF ENCOURAGEMENT: *As Christians we do not have all the answers to life's difficult questions. Nor do we, as golfers, understand exactly how the mind and body work in tandem with a club to send a ball consistently toward a desired target. But we have the comfort of knowing we will get all of our questions answered in eternity.*

I don't know about you, but the first thing I want to do when I reach heaven is to talk to the Lord one on one and ask a few questions. My queries will focus on the reasons for life's tests and trials, not the game.

Others insist, with a smile on their lips, that heaven will include all the greatest golf courses, and they'll hit the links first. After all, heaven wouldn't be paradise without the joy and challenges of playing the game.

One frigid, overcast day — a most unlikely one to discuss the radiance of such mysteries — these words seeped through the bark of the seven cypresses. The wind carried its glorious melody off the land to the sea, whose gray waves paraded to shore like ducklings behind their mother.

> *Dear young cypress sapling,*
>
> *the smallest of any tree*
>
> *not equaling our height*
>
> *but hoping to grow as tall.*
>
> *You ponder your existence,*
>
> *how wind and wave began,*
>
> *how a loving God*
>
> *could make all you see.*

The land, the sky, the animals,

that about us daily live,

calling earth, sky and branches

their one and only home.

Know young cypress that no one

can answer what you ponder.

This being how He planned it,

only praises can we sing.

This being how He planned it,

only praises can we sing.

Animals of all kinds came to hear the splendid song the old cypresses sang. They nestled at the foot of their grizzled trunks, among the sturdy root tops that dug deep into the fertile soil. Animals that moments before preyed upon one another, encircled the trees. There, side by side, were hawks and field mice, coyotes and fawns, foxes and rabbits. And many others whose names I did not know, only that they were predator and prey.

Key Verse — Isaiah 11:6

The wolf will live with the lamb, the leopard will lie down with the goat, the calf and the lion and the yearling together…

On Course

When God's word enters the hearts of Believers prejudices give way to love, allowing natural enemies to set aside their differences and coexist. The game of golf can serve the same purpose in a lesser capacity; giving even complete strangers a common bond that can serve as a foundation for friendship that transcends race, religion, color, creed and class.

All of them were motionless, their eyes wide with wonder as they listened to the cypresses sing about the unexplained mysteries of nature and a loving God amongst us.

The mysteries were of such magnitude that the discussion continued, at least amongst the eldest trees, long after the animals had returned to maintaining the balance of nature.

PART 3

Of Storms & God's Creation

PART THREE
Of Storms & God's Creation

I heard tales about the mystery of storm and of lightning; how these two were born, driven and grew. I learned that bolts that plummeted from dark foreboding clouds were the tree's one mortal enemy. Lightning could shatter even the mightiest sequoia and turn it into a pile of charred rubble. Allowing the sky to obliterate in seconds what had taken the earth generations to nurture from a solitary seed.

KEY TO A CONCLUSION: *What type of event in a Christian's life can destroy his/her faith, do such irreparable damage that the Believer turns his or her back on God? What can a Christian do to regain his/her faith after it's gone?*

27

Usually when a person loses faith in God it is because of a deep personal tragedy, one that leaves the Christian questioning his Creator. "If there is a loving God," he or she might ask, "how could he allow a thing like this to happen?"

Key Verse — Romans 8:28

And we know that in all things God works for the good of those who love him, who have been called according to his purpose.

KEY OF ENCOURAGEMENT: *Often the purpose of tragedy is hidden from us. We must seek the Lord through prayer and ask for the strength, courage, encouragement, wisdom and insight — not to mention the faith needed — to continue, to go forward in life without losing faith in Him and His love for us. Remember, just because it feels like God is no longer there, doesn't mean He isn't.*

Suggestion: *Read the book of Job.*

On Course

What single shot can cause a golfer to lose his or her confidence or faith in his golf game?

The answer: "the 'S' word," S-H-A-N-K, for those of you who can't force yourself to say it. The remedy is to find a PGA professional, take a lesson and learn the cause.

Then work on your swing to eliminate it. And after having done so, your "faith" in your swing will return.

I felt great fear when the elders spoke of the thunderbolts that fell from the sky. The old cypresses knew of the power and danger inherent in lightning, but were unafraid. I found this hard to understand too.

Key Verse — 2 Corinthians 12:10
That is why, for Christ's sake, I delight in weaknesses, in insults, in hardships, in persecutions, in difficulties. For when I am weak, then I am strong.

KEY TO A CONCLUSION: How are we as Christians made strong from becoming weak? What is Paul saying to the Corinthians?

On Course

On a recent installment of "Golf Talk Live," — a segment on The Golf Channel where ex-host Peter Kessler interviewed the world's best golfers — Peter asked Masters champion Bernhard Langer: "Is it true you actually pray on the golf course?"

Bernhard responded and said something like, "Yes. Before I hit a shot I pray for the courage to do it."

At the risk of putting words in Mr. Langer's mouth, I think what he was saying was that he realizes he is weak and needs to draw on God's strength to confront and overcome the situations he faces on the golf course. And needless to say, that would apply equally well in the course of living out our daily lives.

I had seen bolts of light leap from clouds over the sea, but one had never struck the ground nearby. Thunder rolled, making it sound as if the sky was being rent. But I knew enough from my early growth to realize that noises are not to be feared, only what causes them.

Like autumn leaf falling upon autumn leaf after being released from their tree, year piled upon year. The elders love for their creator grew as my bark turned gray, my furrows and braids became deeper and larger. My whole tree gained greater knowledge of God. And I learned about the cycles of life and death among the animals that lived nearby, that every living thing has its beginning and end, is born and must die.

Key Verse — Ecclesiastes 3:1-2, 14
There is a time for everything, and a season for every activity under heaven: a time to be born and a time to die, a time to plant and a time to uproot…

On Course

As seasons come and go and the years roll on, there is time for us as golfers to gather wisdom about ourselves, golf swings and the game itself. Many a golfer, after years of playing the game has commented, "I sure wish I had all the knowledge I have now about the game back when I was just a beginner."

Perhaps it is time you shared some of that knowledge with a fledgling golfer. Chances are someone took the time to do the same for you.

More importantly, take time during your next round to share Christ with a fellow golfer. You will already be standing on acres of common ground.

The fox returned to the grove occasionally to tell me more about the Father, as did the bird with many browns. And in spring, both creatures brought their offspring to the grove — kits and hatchlings that would replace their parents.

Deep in my memory is a lovely clear spring day, the ocean and sky opening up their emerald and pastel blue vistas for miles. Five brown birds visited my tree, the sparkle in their eyes true to that of their parent. The first born told me the sad news of a life lost. Their mother, the one who had danced across my bark and told me of

God's love, had died. But they rejoiced because the Creator cared so deeply for each and every feather of the one whom perished.

Key Verse — Matthew 10:29-31
Are not two sparrows sold for a penny? And yet not one of them will fall to the ground apart from the will of your Father. And even the very hairs of your head are all numbered. So don't be afraid; you are worth more than many sparrows.

KEY OF ENCOURAGEMENT: This scripture says that God loves us so much that He knows the number of the hairs on our heads. Or in my case, what the count is down to after I take a shower each day! When you compare God's knowledge of us — and the love He has for each human — with that of our love for our spouse, children or closest friends, the latter pales in comparison.

On Course

Does God know exactly how many strokes you took during your last round of golf? Of course! Does He equate the amount of strokes you take with your self-worth? Never! Why should you? When your game drags you down, remember God's unconditional love for you apart from it.

Bathed together in sunshine, perched shoulder to shoulder upon me, they warbled a song God must have given them.

Seasons come and seasons go,

soaring inside His will.

Abundant is what our lives will be,

And we will not know fear.

For God abides inside this land,

as does His loving Son.

So dear limb do not dismay,

our mother no longer lives.

Her song has fallen silent now,

but her love lives on in us.

Key Verse — John 13:35

All men will know that you are my disciples if you love one another.

KEY TO A CONCLUSION: *Should Christ's love, "Live on in us"? Did Christ's command for us to love other, even those we consider enemies, include teaching those younger or new to the faith to do the same?*

On Course

Golf is a game that has survived for more than 500 years since its modest birth along the windswept coast of Scotland. In order for it to continue, we need to tell those coming behind us the reasons why we love the sport. Without explaining the game's challenges, skill requirements, and that the game is a metaphor for the Christian life, it will become purely a pursuit of lower scores and a means to win money.

PART 4

Separation in the
Midst of a Storm

PART FOUR
Separation in the Midst of a Storm

Numerous storms had swept in from the sea; towering white thunderheads turned gray and darkened to an ominous black as they piled up against an invisible wall above the ocean. Roaring shoreward, they churned the ocean into an angry, thrashing torrent before engulfing the other cypresses and I in a cool invigorating downpour. During these times even loud claps of thunder caused little fear, though the winds that accompanied the storms were strong enough to tax any tree's limbs.

One spring night, when a full yellow moon hung high in the midnight blue sky and was reflected on the surface of the glassy sea, storm clouds gathered in an enormous huddle out over the ocean. Even in the moonlight, I could see that these clouds held a great deal of strength, a ferocity far greater than I had ever witnessed.

37

The ocean waters rippled in fear under the force of the gale that ran before them. The wind sent the pieces of light that made up the moon's reflection scurrying in all directions like a family of rabbits scattering in the shadow of a swooping hawk.

Following the wind's lead, the clouds began their march toward shore, blinding explosions inside them marking each stride.

I felt no fear at first. I convinced myself that the tempest was not meant for me; that the knowledge of a loving god would prevent the tumultuous events of nature from reaching me and all that I loved.

KEY TO A CONCLUSION: *Does knowing Christ as your personal Savior keep you from experiencing trials and tests? Have you ever heard of the so-called "Prosperity Gospel" (after you accept Christ you will prosper)?*

Key Verse — John 16:33

I have told you these things, so that in me you might have peace. In this world you will have trouble. But take heart! For I have overcome the world.

KEY TO ENCOURAGEMENT: *Yes, we will have trials. But Christ promises repeatedly that He will be with us in* them. And by enduring them with His strength, we will become more like Him. "Prosperity Gospel"? Sounds great. But there's no such thing found in the scriptures. On the contrary, when we become Christians we are asking to endure the fires of adversity. Because it is only in the flames of trial that we can become more like our Savior.

On Course

You can get on the internet, punch in the name of one of those discount golf stores, go to their site and order the latest iron, metal-wood, or hybrid golf club. No matter what clubs you use you will wind up in hazards from time to time. To say that the type of "sticks" you use will keep you from being tested on the golf course is the same as assuming that accepting Christ as Savior will rescue you from the tribulations of life. And you know what happens when you "assume!"

As the storm slammed into the shoreline and our head-dresses began to sway in the breeze, I could no longer deny my fate. My bark prickled with fear as the ocean roared against the rocks far below our plain; the two engaged in a fierce battle for control of the shoreline.

Thunder rumbled through the fabric of the sky, threatening to rend it; how far away the peace of sunny summer afternoons seemed now.

KEY TO A CONCLUSION: *What kind of peace is Christ talking about here? Is it present even when storms in life and on the golf course threaten?*

On Course

Whether we play "Army Golf" (hit shots left-right, left-right), have a case of the snap hooks or can't stop shanking it, we can have peace. For it is not dependent on circumstances on or off the course.

Lightning turned the desolate blackness into flashes of frightening day that revealed nature in frenzy.

The elders, their twisted limbs groaning as they fought the force of the gale, shouted above the howling wind that I should not fear, only trust.

A Grateful Heart

Be thankful for your ability to trust. Without it you could not play golf, nor could you have a personal relationship with Jesus Christ.

Before I could ask what they meant, a white-hot bolt of light dove from the sky directly overhead and tore into the ground. The earth shuddered and quaked. Panic gripped my bark. A deafening clap of thunder rang out and tumbled away.

Another bolt fell. Its searing edge ripped into me. Sparks flew. I was struck, shattered. My branches exploded and rained down on the grove. One blinding, scorching blow severed me from the glorious young cypress where I had grown for countless seasons.

I lay on the ground, decimated. The part of me that held my heart was no bigger than an oversized twig, the same size as the leaves and small strands of wood that lay in a thick mat around the elders. The end of me that had been so gracefully attached to the trunk of my tree was gone.

As I lay upon the ground, one of my ends burned, causing pain that cannot be explained or described. Rain began to fall — preventing fire from consuming what was left of me. In the far reaches of my wood, I hoped desperately for an end to the shower. Death, I thought, would be far better than living apart from my tree.

Key Verse — 2 Corinthians 1:3-7

Praise be to the God and Father of our Lord Jesus Christ, the Father of compassion and the God of all comfort, who comforts us in all our troubles, so that we can comfort those in any trouble with the comfort we received from God. For just as the sufferings of Christ flow over into our lives, so also through Christ our comfort overflows. If we are distressed, it is for your comfort and salvation; if we are comforted, it is for your comfort, which produces in you patient endurance of the same sufferings we suffer.

A Grateful Heart

Even when our trials get so difficult that we do not want to face them — even see death as an option — God is not only there to comfort, but promises that they serve several purposes. One such purpose is to help us understand the sufferings of others, and to share the comfort God gave us with other Believers. Praise God that He comforts us when we need it the most.

On Course

If you've played much golf you've probably had your share of bad rounds. When you play poorly in competition or even in fun and have to face your peers, most of which played better, you will likely dread it. Not so with our loving Father. He will always be there to comfort you no matter what number you shoot.

When one of your friends shoots a bad score when it really counts, pass on the comfort that God gave you by comforting him or her.

Yet, for the first time since I had risen from it, I reveled in the soil I had come from, my birthplace. But my sorrow and pain were so great that joy did not, could not last long.

As the lightning danced in the heavens, I looked up at the cypress I had been so elegantly joined to just moments before, and was swept into a deep chasm of despair and fear.

Key Verse — Isaiah 41:10

So do not fear, for I am with you; do not be dismayed for I am your God. I will strengthen you and help you; I will uphold you with my righteous right hand.

KEY TO ENCOURAGEMENT: When God closes one door he opens another. When one path is blocked He leads us another way. When life forces us to make a clean break with our past or present circumstances, God can lead us in ways we have never dreamt of. His plan for our lives is never devoid of purpose.

Though it is difficult not to fear in times such as these, God says that we simply do not have to.

On Course

If you've played golf for very long you know that there are certain buzz words or phrases that exist. One of those is "comfort zone." This "zone" is the area we are comfortable playing golf in. For instance, if you normally shoot 85 to 90 and are in the middle of the back nine on pace for an 87, you feel comfortable. However, if you have never broken 80 in your life and find yourself standing on the 13th tee three over for the day, chances are you'll be nervous and perhaps fearful that you'll blow your chance to shoot in the 70's.

Remember one thing: (credited to Jack Nicklaus, supposedly after he won the 1986 Masters) "Shaking hands can still make putts."

My branches, with their part in my tree's headdress, were gone. And so was my life with the cypresses.

The storm did not end with the divorce from the tree I loved above all else. As soon as the lightning left the sky and the rain let up, I was pelted by hailstones; hit repeatedly by objects I could neither see coming nor avoid.

The earth muddied beneath me and the wind hurried through the remaining trees, just as questions, carried on frigid winds of doubt, raced through me. Why? Why was this happening to me?

Key Verse — 1 Peter 4:12-14

Dear friends, do not be surprised at the painful trial you are suffering, as though something strange were happening to you. But rejoice that you participate in the sufferings of Christ so that you may be overjoyed when his glory is revealed.

KEY TO A CONCLUSION: *Should you be surprised when you suffer conflicts and difficulties in life?*

On Course

Should we be surprised if we have a bad hole or even a string of them? It happens to all of us, even the pros. "Give me proof!" you say? Jack Nicklaus once shot 82 at Pebble Beach on a picture perfect day.

Realize that this occurrence is common to all that play the game, get less upset when it happens, and play better golf as a result.

Equilibrium returned to our enclave by dawn and the puddle-strewn earth was once again the moist rich soil from which I had come. In the early morning light of a fog-laden dawn I saw the devastation wrought by the storm. The bolt of light had struck precisely where I had been joined to my tree. Parts of me — my branches, twigs and leaves — were scattered everywhere. Only a black burn scar on the bark of my young cypress home recorded my existence.

It was long into that day before I could think of anything but the pain of the separation. During that time, the elders must have noticed what had happened. As white clouds floated and glistened in an azure sky, the elders gave this song to me, a melody of encouragement that brought only confusion to my wood.

You once were part of a grove,

a cypress beside the sea.

But a storm has released you,

so that your faith can grow.

It is not easy to part

with what you dearly love.

It is not easy to know

the depth of God's great care.

But from this place go forth,

to become what He desires.

My respect of the elders for their wisdom was as high and wide as the sky. But as I glanced up at the cypress I once grew from, what little trust I had placed in the God of my elders was put to a strenuous test. As part of a living, thriving tree, I had delighted simply in the passing of days. But in my newfound isolation and aloneness, morning seemed to equal a season, night an eternity in darkness.

KEY OF ENCOURAGEMENT: *Ever been in severe pain? If you have then you know that there are no adjectives to describe just how slowly time passes. Find comfort in the key verses already mentioned. And know that God's strength can help you overcome any discomfort, no matter how long it lasts.*

On Course

Have injuries ever forced you to give up golf for a time? If you've found your way back out on the course, chances are you've discovered a newfound appreciation for the game.

Always hold on to it and never take the game for granted.

If you've had to give up the game completely, perhaps you can find solace in putting and chipping or watching the game on television.

A Grateful Heart

Thank God for all the rounds you have completed in your golfing life and all the unforgettable shots you have hit. Even if you can no longer play, praise God that you had the chance. And for the changes that were wrought in you because you played the noblest game on the planet.

I was still near the cypress tree I had grown from and the other trees were close by. But I was no longer truly a part of the grove.

The shade from the other branches was as cool and refreshing as I imagined mine to be when I provided it, but the words of the elders still made no sense. How could this newborn separation, painful as it had been, cause me to grow and mature?

Was I ever to know a faith, a trust that allowed the grove to welcome even the worst of storms?

Key Verse — James 1:2-5

Consider it pure joy, my brothers, whenever you face trials of many kinds, because you know that the testing of your faith develops perseverance. Perseverance must finish its work so that you may be mature and complete, not lacking anything.

On Course

So, are you supposed to wear a big smile after you double-bogey three holes in a row and ruin the best round of the season? Or worse, make a couple of bad swings and finish "out of the money" when your livelihood depends on the score you shoot? Nope.

But if you do intend on becoming a well-rounded golfer, then you must dig deep and never give up when things go bad. Remember that golf is the most fickle of sports, and as quickly as things take a turn for the worst, they can take a turn for the better — if you **keep trying**!

In short, if your game is tested by bad holes, you develop the perseverance to continue and try to make the round into a respectable one. And by learning the skill of turning a bad round into a good one, you become a more complete and mature player. And eventually you will be glad, maybe even rejoice over what coming back from a few bad holes has taught you.

PART 5

Taken from the Grove

PART FIVE
Taken from the Grove

Springtime had become my favorite of the seasons. Birds were on the wing, excitedly telling of their coming broods; the next generation that would take flight and join with God's nature. Fur-coated animals told of their coming litters too, as orange, lavender and gold wild flowers opened their silken petals wide to drink in the morning dew and ocean mists and to release their sumptuous scents to the ocean breezes that strolled by.

On a cloudy morning almost two months after my terrifying separation in the midst of the storm, a large gray and white bird rode the winds along the coast and circled high above our grove. With each loop the bird dropped lower, its head wagging back and forth like a predator in search of prey.

She continued her descent and, soaring just feet above our grove, made a final pass and landed on the ground near where I had come to rest. Turning her head quickly to and fro, she bent down and scooped up withered grasses and leaves with her slender yellow beak until it looked as if not one more blade could be added. By the way she moved and the look of concern in her eyes, I knew she must have been gathering materials to build a nest.

Beak full to overflowing, she jumped skyward, snapped open her wings in preparation for flight, then tucked them back in. Landing near my side, she bent her head down, cocked it to one side as if wary about picking up a piece of wood my size, and took me in her beak!

Every fiber left within me was saturated with fear. Was this bird going to pluck me from the only home I had ever known?

Key Verse — John 10:29

My Father, who has given them to me, is greater than all; no one can snatch them out of my hand.

KEY TO ENCOURAGEMENT: *If you are pulled from one set of circumstances only to face something more difficult, God will be with you in it.*

You make a triple bogey on one hole and must stand on the next tee — the most difficult hole on the course — and execute one of your best shots of the day. Ask God for the courage to carry out the task. And know He is with you.

Some grass slipped from her grasp as she laid hold.

The bird again jumped toward the sky, spread her pearl white wings and flapped furiously. Her effort to leave the grove was so great that the air rushing in and out of her beak sounded like winter winds locked inside a tempest.

Down below the elders fell away with dizzying speed as the gull caught a rising draft of air in her wingspan. My life as part of a cypress grove was gone. Its memory faded and was replaced by a hope that perhaps there was a reason for this change.

Key Verse — Isaiah 40:31
...but those who hope in the Lord will renew their strength. They will soar on wings like the eagles...

The gull flew ocean ward, holding me firmly but with tender care. Could this be anything like what the elders had once described as being "Held in His hand?"

Grass and wild flowers raced by in a blur beneath us as we dove and flew low to them, the scene fell behind and away as we encountered salty sea breezes over an ocean of blue water. Did this bird live on the other side of the ocean? From what I had learned in the cypress grove, I knew this could not be so. Yet the wings of the feathered creature carried us determinedly out to sea.

Following the length of time it takes the sun to drop below the horizon once it has touched it, the mighty seabird turned and we soared along the land's border. Below the waves frothed, and the surf surged against the massive coastal rocks, making a noise I knew only as a distant roar when I had been part of the grove.

The sadness of separation was left behind with the elders as I saw things they had told me about and more: sea lions, their barks echoing off the nearby cliffs from craggy islands near shore; sea otters playing among the kelp beds; and huge creatures farther out to sea that moved like monstrous shadows inside the deep.

Key Verse: Psalm 104:24-25
How many are your works, O Lord! In wisdom you made them all; the earth is full of your creatures. There is the sea, vast and spacious, teeming with creatures beyond number — living things both large and small.

KEY TO A CONCLUSION: *Could one of God's purposes for bringing loss into our lives have something to do with getting us to see life from His perspective, from a higher point of view?*

Often we are so caught up in our routines that we observe the world from where we stand rather than from where God sits. In being torn away from what we know, we may learn things about God and ourselves that we never knew existed.

Seeing all this reinforced my belief in a benevolent Creator.

KEY TO A CONCLUSION: *As simple as it sounds, seeing any living creature is a reminder to us of God's creative power. Remember that the next time you venture out onto your favorite course.*

Oh, to return to what I used to be so that I could share these new insights!

On Course

Imagine that you have been given the opportunity to go back in time and play a round with yourself as a junior golfer. And that you can pass on all the experience and wisdom you've gleaned from the game.

What would you tell yourself? If you've only been playing golf for several months and could make a similar trek, what advice would give yourself?

The gull started her descent toward dark outcroppings at the ocean's edge. Her brown eyes were fixed on the cliffs laced with terraces and ledges skillfully cut by nature and used for nesting.

As we continued our descent, I learned that the seabird's nest was among a vast colony perched on the cliffs below. At last! Finally I knew my real purpose; to become part of a nest that would shelter a bird's hatchlings. His creatures! Joy as pure as the dawn's first light filled me. I was so elated, so filled with joy, that it would have taken my entire branch to bear it if I was still part of a tree.

Key Verse — James 4:13-16

Now listen you who say, "Today or tomorrow we will go to this or that city, spend a year there and make money." Why, you do not even know what will happen tomorrow. What is your life? You are a mist that appears for a little while and then vanishes. Instead, you ought to say, "If it is the Lord's will, we will live and do this or that." As it is you boast and brag. All such boasting is evil.

KEY TO A CONCLUSION: *How often are we guilty of running ahead of God and doing our own will instead of His? What should be our approach instead?*

On Course

How many times do we as golfers get a good round going, get within a few holes of the clubhouse and determine what our score will be if we par out? The result: usually disastrous. The solution: the old adage: "Take one shot at a time."

Before her webbed feet could touch home, a gust of wind filled her flawless wings and I was jarred free. Wind rushed over me as I plummeted downward, my world spinning and blurred as I tumbled end over end. Splashing into the icy cold water, I tasted the bitterness of ocean salt for the first time.

Shocked by the new sensations, I managed an upward glance. Near the top of the cliff, I saw the silhouette of the mother gull against the deep blue sky. For a long time she just stared at me bobbing about in the water, and finally this came to me:

> *Twig you traveled far,*
>
> *over land, above water to cliff.*
>
> *I, a gull, regret*

you couldn't be of my nest.

If I'd tried to save you,

to catch you in the air,

I would have dropped the grass,

I found amongst the trees.

It is all too clear,

my nest could not be your home.

But on the sea you'll go,

on its waters wander.

I had been severed from my tree. And the glory of flight that I was certain would end in purposefulness was over.

The Grand One had told of dreams lost and found. One quiet summer afternoon he explained that those who believed in God and "Accepted and trusted Christ as Savior often discovered a meaning and purpose for their existence they never dreamt of before they knew Him."

I chose to accept and trust.

Key Verse — John 3:16

For God so loved the world that he gave us his one and only Son, that whoever believes in him would not perish but have everlasting life.

PART 6

Out to Sea

PART SIX
Out to Sea

Dozens of gulls returned from their inland flights; flying over the emerald waters near to the cliffs with beaks full of grasses and leaves. The calls that fell from their beaks to the surface of the sea spoke of homes being readied for hatchlings.

In the heart of my wood I hoped that one of them would pull me from my uncertainty, but none did. Currents pulled me from the base of the cliffs and the land was swallowed by a watery horizon inside the light of that day.

As a cypress limb, I had heard little about the sea. All I knew had been given to me by the elders whose knowledge came from animals that lived along its edge. The Grand One had told me of its length, while the rest of the grove compared its depth to God's love for us all.

> **Key Verse — Ephesians 3:17-19**
> And I pray that you, being rooted and established in love, may have power together with all the saints, to grasp how wide and long and high and deep is the love of Christ…

KEY OF ENCOURAGEMENT: *It is reassuring to know that God loves us so much that the very dimensions of His love are difficult to grasp. And, according to this scripture, it takes the prayers of other Believers to make comprehending His love possible.*

Don't ever forget this facet of God's love, especially when you are severely tested in life or on the golf course.

Weeks stretched into months. Seasons passed and came again. I learned that nowhere is God more evident than at sunset, when even a tiny piece of driftwood can be awed by the amber, gold and lavender clouds that waft above the horizon, the whole scene reflected toward the sky by a placid sea.

> **Key Verse — Psalm 50:1**
> The Mighty One, God, the Lord, speaks and summons the earth from the rising of the sun to the place where it sets.

ιought of The Grand One and his infinite wisdom, because now I knew things about the land and the sea that he had not been allowed to experience. Could it be that this was the lesson of separation, as difficult and as devastating as it had been?

Key Verse — Proverbs 4:7

Wisdom is supreme; therefore get wisdom. Though it cost you all you have, get understanding.

KEY TO A CONCLUSION: *Why is it that gaining wisdom can be costly? In life we can make mistakes that are painful to ourselves and to those around us. But errors in judgment allow us to learn or gain wisdom so that we do not make the same mistakes again.*

Does God teach us spiritual lessons in the same manner by using our mistakes to grow us into Believers that more closely resemble his Son?

On Course

As manager of shoe and locker room services at an opulent country club in Arizona, I have been given the privilege of playing a world class golf course that presents its share of challenges to the golfer. The 6th hole, a downhill par 4 of 452 yards from the black or back tees, is the toughest hole on the course.

While the drive doesn't present much of a problem, the approach is where the men get separated from the boys and the women from the girls. To the right of the green are a series of huge yawning bunkers waiting to gobble up your ball. To the left is what is called "manicured desert," another term for what looks like the remains of a dirt road. Following about five yards of that is the real desert-scrub brush, creosote bushes, and cacti.

As if that wasn't enough, a mound that will throw any ball rolling toward it into the bunkers or desert fronts the green. That is unless you hit the ball near the center of the mound and there's enough on it to chase the little rascal onto the green.

And finally, more often than not you are forced to hit the troublesome approach from an uneven lie.

My strategy the first several times I played the hole was to ignore the pin and hit the approach, usually requiring a long iron or fairway wood — for me anyway — right at the center of the green. I paid the price when I pulled my shot and ended up with a bogey, double-bogey or worse. I eventually learned — gained enough wisdom to realize — that if I was going to miss the green it would have to be in the bunkers and not on the short side. At least from the sand I had a chance of making par and most of the time no worse than bogey.

Utilizing my ability to work the ball, I now get over the approach shot, aim for the middle of the green and set up for a fade. By doing so I take the left side out of play; I haven't been left in weeks. And have even made a birdie or two on the 6th in the last couple of months.

What can you do to gain wisdom and play better on the toughest hole on your course? Or at least on the one you score highest on? If you don't know, ask a PGA professional. You may not be advanced enough to work the ball, but there are many other ways to make a good score on a hole that "has your number."

I drifted on, land still unknowable. I saw many dawns and dusks alone, my sojourn in solitude unbroken until, beneath a black night sky sprinkled with blazing white stars, something enormous rose out of the dark still waters. The same color as the water that held me, it looked as if the sea was bulging toward the sky.

Bubbles wider than the wingspan of a condor rose from the depths. As they reached the surface of the sea they burst open and words, somehow trapped inside, gave themselves up.

> Driftwood, driftwood,
>
> I am the whale.
>
> I may be large,
>
> many times your weight.
>
> But we are equals,
>
> in God's loving eyes.

Key Verse — 1 John 3:1
How great is the love the Father has lavished on us, that we should be called children of God!

KEY OF ENCOURAGEMENT: *It is encouraging to know that no matter our status, race, color, creed or even our size, that God loves all of us equally and sees us as so precious to Him that He calls us His "children."*

KEY TO A CONCLUSION: *Have you ever stopped to wonder what God must think of the game of golf? Better yet, how would Christ play the game? I am not attempting to be funny or disrespectful here.*

No matter what your response to the above questions is, you can rest assured that we are not judged by how far we can belt a drive or how many putts we can make in the "throw up zone (inside six feet)." God looks upon the heart, not the swing.

A Grateful Heart

Praise God that we don't have to golf our way into heaven! Could you imagine standing over a five-footer in front of the pearly gates with your eternal destiny hanging in the balance? Make it and stroll into eternal bliss. Miss and suffer unspeakable damnation that never ends. The ultimate pressure putt!

Instead all we have to do is accept Christ as Savior. A free gift that is dependent on nothing except our willingness to embrace it.

> *So do not fear,*
>
> *as you drift on.*
>
> *The sea is home to many,*
>
> *of plankton and me.*

I thanked the whale for his encouragement and the bony, barnacle-covered hump disappeared into the water, leaving behind tiny whirlpools that captured and gave up the starlight.

In the stillness of the passing days, as I drifted upon the rolling waters that stretched to every horizon, I thought often of the many seasons I had grown amongst the deeply rooted cypresses. I thought too about how my green, fragrant leaves formed part of my cypress's headdress, and captured the sunlight and raindrops to sustain my tree.

And how, because of my wanderings, my old bark had fallen away. I now saw the world in a new way through unprotected wood.

Key Verse — 2 Corinthians 5:17
Therefore, if anyone is in Christ he is a new creation; the old has gone and the new has come!

KEY TO A CONCLUSION: *Am I suggesting that after you accept Christ you go from a thriving individual to being, "dead in the water"? Far from it! If you know Christ your life takes on newness and an exciting sensitivity to God's purposes as you live for Him. And use your gifts to benefit the church and build His kingdom on earth.*

I was a fragment of the limb I took so long to become, now graying and soggy as I bobbed in and to places unknown.

Instead of fearing storms like the one that caused the separation from my tree, they became adventures that I welcomed. Driven by gale winds, tall ravenous waves would rise, bare their teeth and bite down hard upon me. I took the tests one at a time and simply floated in and through them.

Key Verse — Matthew 6:34

Therefore do not worry about tomorrow, for tomorrow will worry about itself. Each day has enough trouble of its own.

On Course

Discipline your mind to stay on the shot at hand and then when done, move onto the next. This mindset, whether dealing with the storms of life or the next shot on the golf course, is the same. Literally take one day at a time and don't allow yourself to think of any other trials that must be faced except for those inside that day. And take one swing at a time when playing golf.

Do not allow your mind to wander ahead to the next shot, the next hole, or the 19th hole. You'll do better in life and golf if you do.

KEY TO A CONCLUSION: Why is it that Christ admonished us to "Take one 'day' at a time," and the golf gurus suggest we "Take one 'shot' at a time?"

Lightning and thunder above the sea were no less powerful than over the land. Bolts of light that dwarfed any I'd seen above the elders dove seaward to light up the writhing, frigid waters in the dark of night. Thunder tore through the sky following each bolt of light here too. But without the land and trees to catch the sounds, it spread across the sky in every direction like a thick, deafening fog.

All of this was simply a demonstration of God's power and majesty. Why could I not think of Him in this way before the separation?

On Course

Tests, both on the course and off, take on a new meaning when Believers realize they serve a purpose and actually benefit them by growing their faith. As a result, the mature Christian does not fear trials, but comes to see them as a means of drawing closer to God and becoming more like his Son. However, it often takes time and life experience to recognize this truth.

Therefore, as noted earlier in the book, it is possible to rejoice when they occur. Not easy! But as Philippians 4:13 says, "I can do everything through him who gives me strength." Golfers, on the other hand, mature if they learn from mistakes that cause high numbers and realize that if they are again confronted with the same set of circumstances that caused the bad scores, they can make better choices. By doing so, they come to trust more in their "golfing judgment."

After wandering for a time that I could not measure, the eastern horizon gave birth to land, to a coastline that rose slowly and gracefully on a distant edge of my world.

During my first few weeks at sea, as God's embroidered skies glowed at dawn and at dusk, I had prayed that I might wash ashore on a white sandy beach. A shore where I could lay in comfort near the wise cypress grove I once called home.

Key Verse — John 14:14

You may ask me for anything in my name, and I will do it.

Key Verse — 1 John 5:14-15

This is the assurance we have in approaching God: that if we ask anything according to his will, he hears us.

A place with trees knowledgeable about God and the character of Christ, no matter the name they were known by.

The shoreline stole more of the cloudless sky as I neared the land. But the sun, a fiery red ball at day's end, sank and darkness arrived before I was able to touch the beach I longed for.

As the sun rose to meet a small flock of clouds on the horizon, I found myself closer to the white sandy beach, a pristine shoreline like the one I had dreamt of. To my dismay, I found it stoutly guarded by craggy brown rocks that stood defiantly in the shallows. While waves, washing up on the sandy shore, whispered as they turned into glassy sheets.

Caught in the clutch of a strong curling wave, the water gave me this as I went dizzy.

> *Driftwood, driftwood,*
>
> *long out to sea,*
>
> *you now find yourself*

caught in a wave.

Will you tumble,

in waves to the sand?

Or stay in the shallows

to change still more?

Reeling inside the wave, I slammed into something immovable, one of the craggy rocks near shore. Caught in a backwash as wave after wave rolled relentlessly toward shore, I was thrown against it again and again and again. Chunks were being cut out of me. My surface was nicked and pitted, creating a roughness like the bark I once owned.

I had come so far. I had learned so much. I had gained such faith. I could not understand another battering, one that I could not escape.

Key Verse — 2 Corinthians 11:25-28

Five times I received from the Jews the forty lashes minus one. Three times I was beaten with rods, once I was stoned, three times I was shipwrecked, I spent a day and a night in the open sea, I have been constantly on the move. I have been in danger from rivers, in danger from bandits, in danger from my own countrymen, in danger from Gentiles; in danger in the

---

city, in danger in the country, in danger at sea; and in danger from false brothers. I have labored and toiled and often gone without sleep; I have known hunger and thirst and have often gone without food; I have been cold and naked. Besides everything else, I face the daily pressure of my concern for all the churches.

KEY TO A CONCLUSION: *Did Paul ever feel like he couldn't face another battering in the form of beatings or being in some type of peril? If he was human he did. Yet, this was the same man that said, "I eagerly expect and hope that I will in no way be ashamed, but will have sufficient courage so that now as always Christ will be exalted in my body, whether by life or by death. For to me, to live is Christ and to die is gain." Philippians 1:20-21.*

A Grateful Heart

Thank God that we do not have to endure what Paul did for his faith.

On Course

When you play several bad holes in a row or start taking the game a bit too seriously, think about what Paul went through in biblical times. And what

Christians must endure in other countries at present simply for confessing Christ as their Savior.

Golf becomes far less important when compared to life threatening situations brought about by confessing Christ as Savior. It is, in a context such as this, just a game.

At last a large kind wave that was about to crest and fold onto it self tossed me up on a small holding in the rock. From that spot just out of the reach of the waves tumbling shoreward, I saw the particles cut from me floating away in every direction. What purpose could becoming rough again possible serve?

The sea had stripped away my bark and left me smooth during my countless months upon it. And I had become convinced that was how God wanted me to be.

But the water carried away chunks of me. I would have grieved, but the exuberance of resting on this jagged piece of wet, solid earth did not allow it.

I had learned, only because of God's strength, to love the sea and call it home. Great was the wisdom and faith He had given me as I roamed the surface of the waters. But every grain of my wood still longed to be planted and find a home.

Key Verse — Philippians 1:23

I am torn between the two: I desire to depart and be with Christ, which is better by far; but it is more necessary for you if I remain in the body.

Key Verse — 2 Corinthians 5:9

So we make it our goal to please him, whether we are at home in the body or away from it.

KEY TO A CONCLUSION: *Is it safe to say that most Believers can relate to Paul's longing to be with Christ? When life bears down on us and the stresses build, it's only natural to want to be with God. Yet, Paul says that it is in the best interest of those around us to remain here. That is until God decides to take us home to Himself.*

PART 7

Sculpted in the Shallows

80

PART SEVEN
Sculpted in the Shallows

The brown rock, alive with sea grasses and shells, possessed greater wisdom than that of The Grand One. Rock, I soon learned, was not subject to the cycles of life and death as I had come to know them.

We exchanged our knowledge of the loving Father, and the rock, during my stay upon it, taught me this. Words that every sea rock knew:

> *We sea rocks guard land.*
>
> *Counted, we number more*
>
> *than the stars in the heavens.*
>
> *Sparkling, we tell of His love*
>
> *that took Christ to The Hill,*

to Calvary all alone,

that mankind could have faith

solid as a sea rock.

That mankind could have faith

solid as a sea rock.

Key Verse — Psalm 18:2
The Lord is my rock, my fortress and my deliverer; my God is my rock, in whom I take refuge.

A Grateful Heart
Praise God that we serve a Lord that is perfect, just and solid as stone.

The tide returned too soon and lifted me from that weathered rock. I took wisdom with me, leading me to believe that my new roughness had been purposeful.

Meandering toward shore, I could taste permanence as strongly as I did the bitter salt when I had slipped from the grasp of the gull into the icy waters of the sea. Arrival on land would be sweet after a journey not countable in weeks, months or even seasons.

Floating with tantalizing closeness to the shore, I inexplicably found myself headed back out to sea. An unseen force pulled me away from my destination. In my disappointment I drifted with the current, going where God bade me to go as I had for so long. I concluded that if the only lesson I had learned during my sojourn at sea was to ask for and trust in God's wisdom, the time had been well spent.

Key Verse — James 1:5-6
If any of you lacks wisdom, he should ask God, who gives generously to all without finding fault, and it will be given to him.

KEY TO A CONCLUSION: *Does God need to get you alone with Himself — through situations or circumstances — before you will come before Him and ask what He wants you to do? Perhaps that is the very reason God is giving you no other options except to turn to Him for help.*

Still I was burdened with questions, so weighed down that I feared I would sink, and that everything I had learned about God, the sea, and all of its creatures would be shared with no one.

A Grateful Heart

It is reassuring to know that God is willing to share our
burdens when our fear is the greatest, whether it be on
the golf course or off. He also helps us make sense out
of the fear and suffering we experience in both places.

In the quiet stirring of the current I rode, I heard this:

> *I am the riptide*
>
> *pulling back out to sea*
>
> *to cause you to pause,*
>
> *so you will keep your faith.*
>
> *For if you depend*
>
> *on His unending strength,*
>
> *my grip on your wood*
>
> *will not tarry long.*

I went where the current pulled me with no resistance and gave to God the last fiber of my will and strength. After growing, the painful separation, then flying and drifting, placing my hope in Him was all that was left for me to do.

Key Verse — Psalm 147:11
…the Lord delights in those who fear him, who put their hope in his unfailing love.

Key Verse — Psalm 119:116
Sustain me according to your promise, and I will live; do not let my hopes be dashed.

KEY TO A CONCLUSION: *Is God at work in our lives so that we will give up the last vestiges of our right to ourselves and let Him have us wholly and completely? Is God pleased when we surrender all that we are to His will for our lives? Have you pleased God in this way?*

A Grateful Heart
Thank God that because we know Him we will never be without hope no matter how difficult life gets or how badly we score on the golf course.

The riptide must have known my heart and released me to the waves. I tumbled closer to shore as each one passed over me. And the hope that my sogginess would yield to the warming sun grew.

An eternity passed before I first washed up on the shore. Though wet and cold, the sands refreshed me as thoroughly as my first drink of spring rain while I was still inside my seed. For days the waves rolled me up on the sand. And I rolled back with them to stay in the shallows.

As this occurred, I noticed the sand was changing me, wearing my nicked edges smooth and honing away the knots where twigs once grew. It occurred to me that I had been out to sea and turned gray, was battered to roughness by the rock, and was now being smoothened by the sand. Could all this have happened by chance?

Key Verse — Romans 8:28

And we know that in all things God works for the good of those who love him, who have been called according to his purpose.

KEY TO A CONCLUSION: *This passage is quoted often when tragedy strikes. It was quoted earlier in this book and has helped many a Believer make sense out of his circumstances. It has also helped many to know that there are no accidents in our walk with God in life or on the links.*

At the same time we must realize we may not get all the answers as to why God allows certain things to happen to us. Instead we have to believe that our God is in control, and that our character and walk with Christ will be made stronger as a result.

On Course

God is continually shaping us through circumstances, spending time in God's word, prayer and fellowshipping with other Believers. The game of golf is at work in our hearts sculpting who we are by how we react to the shots we hit.

KEY TO A CONCLUSION: Do you complain or always have something negative to say about each shot you make? Do you have a temper that causes you to swear a blue streak, throw balls or break clubs? Are any of these behaviors a true reflection of what our life in Christ should be like?

As I reflected on these thoughts the saturated sands beneath me came alive, answering some of my questions.

Driftwood, driftwood,

you tumble on sand

to be shaped and formed,

and touched by God.

Land that was born

from water shattered rock

that has come here in time

over countless days.

Sand that knows rain

only as tears

like the Lord shed,

as He died on the cross,

so that mankind

could be free from sin.

Key Verse: Romans 6:5-7

If we have been united with him in his death, we will also certainly be united with him in his resurrection. For we know that our old self was crucified with him so that the body of sin might be rendered powerless, that we should no longer be slaves to sin because anyone who has died has been freed from sin.

A Grateful Heart

Praise God for the sacrifice His Son made so that we could be free of sin.

During the days and nights that I spent being shaped, the wet sand and I talked of the open sea and how the land had come to know the water as its friend. That had been the only right choice, it maintained, as both were joined intimately along coastlines without end.

I admitted my puzzlement to the sand and thought, wasn't the sea a foe when it worked in concert with storm to destroy the coastline with the power of wind and wave?

The sand answered gently, possessing knowledge of tempests I had found nowhere else. As had The Grand One and the other cypresses, the sand explained how storms ride upon the sea. That the two do not join in purposeful destruction. It added that storms come also from the land to the sea. And it is then that the land reclaims what the ocean once possessed.

The sand was certain of one thing; storms help to maintain a balance along the coast.

Key Verse — 1 Peter 1:6-7
...though now for a little while you may have to suffer grief in all kinds of trials. These have come so that your faith — of greater worth than gold, which perishes even though refined by fire — may prove genuine and may result in praise, glory and honor when Jesus Christ is revealed.

SCULPTED IN THE SHALLOWS

KEY TO A CONCLUSION: *Do we need trials and tests in our lives to help us maintain a close, balanced relationship with our Lord? If everything in your life is going exceedingly well, what happens to your relationship with God? Does it stay balanced and consistent or do you fall out of close fellowship with Him?*

As part of a young cypress with shallow roots, none of this would have made sense to me. But my survival of many gales at sea proved the sand's wisdom to be the truth. Only after riding out the most horrendous storm did I sincerely appreciate a still sea reflecting clouds afloat in an exquisite blue sky.

On Course

If our golf games never slumped, would we appreciate playing at the top of our game? It is only after a prolonged battle with our golf swing that ends in finding our game that we have a true appreciation for our skills.

A Grateful Heart

Thank God that you have, at times, struggled with your golf game. It makes the days when you have your "'A' Game" all that much more enjoyable.

Perhaps, I thought, it is in journeying rather than growing in one place that God's wisdom and love is found.

KEY TO A CONCLUSION: *Does anyone ever "arrive spiritually"? I can only think of One. Or is the Christian life a continuous process?*

On Course

Has there ever been a professional golfer that has "arrived," has every shot in the bag and no longer needs to practice? Tiger Woods?

Nope. His former teacher, Butch Harmon, once said that Tiger has only reached 75% of his potential. Now there's a scary thought for the rest of the golfing world!

I knew much more than I did when I first plunged into the ocean, but I still dared not think I knew more than The Grand One. His wood, after all, was centuries old.

Key Verse — Romans 12:3

For by the grace given me I say to every one of you: Do not think of yourself more highly than you ought, but rather think of yourself with sober judgment, in accordance with the measure of faith that God has given you.

KEY TO A CONCLUSION: *Is the scripture suggesting that there is no room for self-confidence among Believers? Or are we encouraged to think of ourselves in realistic — sober — terms?*

On Course

The scripture from Romans applies equally well to how we carry ourselves as Christians on the golf course, especially in the heat of competition.

My kinship with the wet sand and the shallows ended in time, but not before my wood was as smooth as a dolphin's tail fin. My deepest nicks were hardly visible and I had grown a shade or two grayer. However, I had yet to find the shore. Instead I came to rest in a shallow tidal pool near the beach.

I lay half in the water and half out, still not completely free of the ocean. There in the tidal pool was what the cypresses had called a starfish. They had recounted it with reverence, and let me know that a star in the heavens had played a role in the story of God's Son.

Unlike any fish I had seen swimming in the open water, it was orange-red, rough, and pointed in five directions. It was far less lively than even the whale; nonetheless, it had seen much in its days.

Its wisdom and love of the Father were as peculiar as its shape, different from that of the cypress trees or even the rock in the shallows. This was borne out by the poem the fish gave me that could be heard far beyond the tidal pool.

Who has wisdom,

wave or stone?

Or is it here,

God made man?

Man that goes

about the sea,

roaming the depths,

with caution spent.

Mankind lives

as it will,

forgetting a Savior

it can trust.

I'd rather live

in a tidal pool

than without Him

inside the deep.

No other creature or object had described mankind and its relationship with Christ as this fish had. The star gave me much wisdom as I shared its pool. He told me about rumbling things that sliced through the surface of the ocean were vessels that carried men He said that they were the Father's creation too and that Christ came robed in flesh as one of them to share his plan of salvation and servant-hood.

The starfish explained how his namesake in the night sky was used by God to draw men called shepherds and kings to a place where the Savior was born. And it conveyed that every man could have a personal relationship with Christ if only he asked the Savior into his heart and believed the Christ was the Son of God.

The tide was beginning to return and would lift me from the pool. My faith had grown immensely from what I'd learned. And I hated to leave because I wanted to know more about the Christ.

Acceptance and trust was no longer enough.

Key Verse — 1 Peter 2:2-3
Like newborn babies, crave spiritual milk, so that by it you may grow up into your salvation, now that you have tasted that the Lord is good.

PART 8

Buried in Darkness & Doubt

PART EIGHT
Buried in Darkness & Doubt

Afloat again in the ocean, I was no longer concerned how long I drifted on the water or when I would reach land. I knew one thing for certain, that no matter where God wanted me, I would find contentment there.

Key Verse — 1 Timothy 6:6-9

But godliness with contentment is great gain. For we brought nothing into this world, and we can take nothing out of it. But if we have food and clothing, we will be content with that.

A Grateful Heart

As Christians, we need to avoid the trap set for us by the world, that we must keep acquiring material things in order to find happiness. This verse clearly says that if we have the basics of food and clothing we should be content. How much more grateful we should be then because we have golf clubs, the skill to use them, and the resources to play golf courses we enjoy.

On Course

Before buying a new set of clubs, or even a new putter or wood, have you ever stopped to ask God if you should be content with what you already have? I know one man who did, and he was given a sense of contentment that arrested his need for a new set of irons.

I finally washed ashore on a beach with soft, white, powdery sand. The kind I had dreamed of resting upon during my entire odyssey. From there I saw many more sunrises and sunsets. Storms came and went; the sand blew and drifted and smoothed out all but a few of my nicks.

Dry, I was far lighter in weight and color than when I was dressed in bark and living leaves. But I was heavy with wisdom and knowledge of God.

KEY TO A CONCLUSION: *What are your sources of wisdom? Life experience? Reading books and magazines? God's Word? Can we ask God for wisdom on and off the course? See James 1:5-6.*

Finally! Finally I had found shore! It was barren soil, but it was soil just the same!

Salt air, carried to my shore by gentle breezes, refreshed and rejuvenated the weary heart that I carried deep in my wood. But the gentle breezes stiffened to winds that conspired with the sand and covered me over. I could no longer see my Creator's dawns and dusks splashed across the sky on clouds of crimson, pink, lavender and gold. Nor could I look to the whispering waves for wisdom. Or hope to hear the story of the birth of Christ from the starfish.

Buried, I knew only black and cold in winter and darkness and sweltering heat in summer. Pressed on every side by sand, I pondered my past. The only thing I knew for certain other than what I had learned about God and the Christ. As I thought about my life on the land and of God, the wind above me whipped into frenzy, the sand skidded over itself, and the two of them, together, gave me ideas that confused and frightened me.

> *Driftwood locked in blackness,*
>
> *buried inside the sand,*
>
> *you pictured a different life*
>
> *once you reached the shore.*
>
> *Life lived in wisdom,*
>
> *God loved with all your wood.*
>
> *But instead you lie in darkness,*
>
> *heat and cold endure.*
>
> *If there is a god,*
>
> *why did you wash ashore?*
>
> *Has His love for driftwood,*
>
> *lost its tender care?*

Key Verse — 1 Peter 5:8,9
Be self-controlled and alert. Your enemy the devil prowls around like a roaring lion looking for some-one to devour. Resist him, standing firm in the faith.

KEY TO A CONCLUSION: *Is Satan out there looking for ways to separate us from our belief in God and His love for us? You bet! Ask God to help you resist him and stand firm in the faith.*

A Grateful Heart
Thank God for his ability to keep us safe from Satan and his attacks upon us.

Though certain God loved all of his creations, the questions pressed hard on my wood like the thousand of grains of sand that held me. I doubted the assurances of The Grand One, the brown bird with the eyes that sparkled, and what had been given me by every creature I had met during my seasons at sea. I even doubted the ancient sea rocks!

Key Verse — Hebrews 10:23
Let us hold unswervingly to the hope we profess, for he who promised is faithful.

KEY OF ENCOURAGEMENT: *During times of stress, grief or loss, it is easy in our humanness to doubt that God exists or even that He cares. It is at times like this that we must decide to remain faithful and remember that nothing can*

separate us from His love. See Romans 8:37-39. He has
remained faithful in the past, present and will be in the future.

On Course

There will be times when our golf swings betray us and we, as golfers, doubt that we will ever play to our ability again. At a time like this it is important to go back to the fundamentals, see a PGA Professional for a golf lesson, and correct the flaws that created the problems you face.

In Dr. Bob Rotella's book, *Golf is a Game of Confidence* (Simon and Schuster, 1995), you will learn what to do if the problem is strictly one of self-assurance and believing in oneself.

All of them knew about a benevolent loving Creator. A resident of a tidal pool had even shared its knowledge of a compassionate Father who sent his only Son to die on an earth He made. I had never stopped to think if what I was told was the truth.

In my endless night imprisoned in the sand, I weighed my experiences against what the sand and wind had put to me in questions. God was real, I thought.

If He wasn't, how could all creatures, from the whale to the starfish, know of His love? How could all of nature balance so intricately? How could my destruction give birth to faith? Separation to wisdom? Battering and sculpting to reshaping and newness?

Key Verse — 1 Corinthians 16:13

Be on your guard; stand firm in the faith; be men of courage; be strong.

KEY TO ENCOURAGEMENT: *No matter the strength of their convictions or the number of years that have passed since coming to Christ, most Christians, at one point or another, have doubts about whether or not God is real.*

Doubts are erased by looking back over the years and realizing the many ways that God has shown himself to be faithful, provided for our needs, and never stopped showing each one of us the depth of His love. Reading God's promises in scripture and talking with mature Christians can also help.

For this reason, doubt is actually a very healthy thing. Because by thinking it through we come to own it, making our faith more personal and more real.

Perhaps the powdered sand had questions of its own, but had decided that a god with boundless grace would never create so much of one thing made up of so many that journeyed so little.

After all, I had known life as a living, breathing tree limb, had flown high above the earth in the tender tether of a seabird and floated effortlessly though the worst storms at sea. The sand had so little to draw from while I had, in turn, been given so much.

KEY TO A CONCLUSION: *Does an individual's life experiences make it easier to come to Christ than those of another person? Does God care about our past or is accepting Him as personal Savior really all that matters?*

Existing inside the sand, sharing intimacy with it for years, the sand and I came to know each other well. After I described my separation and wanderings, the sand used them as proof that there was no Creator.

It claimed that no god, especially one as loving and full of grace as I claimed Him to be, would cause any of His creatures to endure what I had.

Key Verse — Matthew 5:45
He causes the sun to rise on the evil and the good, and sends the rain on the righteous and unrighteous.

KEY TO A CONCLUSION: *Does knowing Christ exempt us from tragedy? If a tornado rips through a town are the Christians spared?*

Somewhere along the line we have learned — or at least heard — that knowing Christ as Savior protects us from the realities of life: death, loss etc. But the Savior's own words, above, quoted out of the gospel of Matthew tell us otherwise. And as has been noted earlier in this book, being a Christian is often more difficult because we are asking to become more like Christ. Unfortunately, He uses trials and adversity to accomplish His goal.

On Course

Have you ever played competitive golf? I played four years of high school golf and four years of college golf. I also played in a number of summer tournaments for junior golfers in and around the town where I grew up.

During a few of my college and high school matches my opponent cursed and slammed his clubs to the ground after any poor shot. Some opponents even tried to break my concentration by utilizing various forms of gamesmanship.

Did I always win my matches against this type of person? I would like to say I did, but I lost my share. Both good and bad things happen to golfers that believe in God, just as rain (trials and tribulations) falls on the righteous and unrighteous.

Yet, the sand was uncertain. Unsure because it had heard the sea stones praise their god in the midst of terrible storms when waves black as night and taller than any tree slammed into them. According to the sand the stones never uttered one word of complaint, and instead praised the storms and mighty waters for sculpting and making them even more faithful to their god.

KEY TO A CONCLUSION: *One of the most powerful tools we have to share our faith — many times without even realizing we're doing it — is our Christian reaction to adversity. Those who refuse to acknowledge the existence of God and salvation through his Son begin to have doubts about their unbelief when they see Christians meet tragedy with tranquility and peace. Or see in the Believer a joy that transcends life circumstances.*

On Course

Obviously, the same example can be set on the golf course. Those of us who belong to Christ should exhibit a peace and joy that rises above the typical reaction to a bad shot or attaches so much significance to what our scorecard reads at the end of 18 holes that a bad day results in a petulant mood. That doesn't mean Believers don't lose their temper or fall into the old trap of attaching self-worth to the score they shoot. It just means we, with God's help, try to be more like Christ each time we tee it up.

> ## Key Verse — Acts 26:28
> Then Agrippa said to Paul, "Do you think that in such a short time you can persuade me to be a Christian?"

KEY TO ENCOURAGEMENT: *Whether you have just started playing golf or have played your entire life, if you don't know Christ, find Him. Don't fail to be persuaded as King Agrippa was.*

There are eternal consequences to your decision.

The sand, discipled by the sea stones and a weary piece of driftwood, came to believe. I was again to see the brilliant glitter of the sun on the surface of the emerald sea. The sand had not confined me because I believed in God and it, at first, did not. But rather that this was another part of the journey that allowed me to grow closer to my Creator.

Time passed, as did the gray whales offshore, making their customary way south. The dolphins, sea lions and otters frolicked in the foam and waves beyond the sea stones. The cycles of life beside the sea followed their own distinct rhythm, but were similar to those I had seen on land.

The ocean, seen after years in the sand, had a beauty and wonder I had taken for granted during my journey upon it. I had spent so much time on the sea that it was like a second home. And there were times when the sand held me that I yearned to see the sun ablaze, poised above a watery horizon, its rays turning clouds to crimson and deep purples.

I also missed the birds that flew over me as I drifted. Each time I saw one I wondered how such a tiny heart could carry the strength and stamina necessary to cross an entire ocean. My conclusion was always the same, that with God anything is possible.

Key Verse — Philippians 4:13
I can do everything through him who gives me strength.

A Grateful Heart
Thank God for all the things that you have accomplished because God gave you the strength to do them, especially surviving the death of a loved one.

For it was God who had created the bird, the gray and white gull that used the winds to glide effortlessly hundreds of feet above me.

PART 9

In Flight on the Wings of Purpose

PART NINE
In Flight on the Wings of Purpose

With wing edges dazzling white against the sun, the gull's intermittent shrieks echoed off the pocked brown cliffs behind me and warned of a visit to the sand. It went into a steep dive, pulled up before smashing into the ground, and flew at me low. Gliding into the incoming breeze, the gull held itself a few feet above me. In its eyes was a message with a sense of certainty.

Driftwood, oh driftwood,

on land and in the light

always recall what happened

as you floated on the sea.

As your bark fell away,

you now see all things new,

111

and you always will

upon the land or in the sea.

Though I hadn't really thought of it in that way, the gull spoke the truth. As had the first brown bird that had landed on my limb and sang of God's love. After all I had seen, after everything God's strength had allowed me to overcome, the change seemed like a lifetime ago.

Key Verse — Ephesians 4:22-24

You were taught with regard to your former way of life, to put off the old self, which is being corrupted by its deceitful desires; to be made new in the attitude of your minds; and to put on the new self, created to be like God in true righteousness and holiness.

On Course

Golf is a game that can alter who we are as we react to the outcome of our golf shots. To reach our potential as players, we must manage our emotions through the ups and downs of even a single round of golf. It is no secret that the winners on any given week on the professional tours are the pros that are not only mechanically sound and have great short games, but are the ones that can stay calm and focused.

As a teenager I had very high expectations of the golf shots I hit. If they didn't come off exactly like I wanted them to I got very angry. In fact, when I was 16 I missed a short putt, walked off the green and buried the putter head in the fringe. When I pulled the club back out, the head stayed planted. When I look back on how much my golf course demeanor has changed since my adolescence, it seems like a different person swung the club. Oh, I still get frustrated at times, but I've learned that golf is just a hobby, albeit a challenging one that will test the most patient man or woman.

Paul is saying the same thing about the spiritual life of the Believer. We are to take off the old self and put on the new. But that doesn't mean we won't stumble.

Have you ever changed your grip or completely overhauled your golf swing? Then you know it takes hard work to stick with the changes. And that you'll fall into your old swing pattern every now and again before the changes become permanent.

A Grateful Heart

Thank God that you have His wisdom and strength to draw on when it comes to changing your self. And that the only true and lasting changes are a result of God's strength and grace.

The seabird caught a rising spiral of air, rose quickly into the sky and turned south to follow the whales. Before the bird left my sight it peered back, winked and nodded. I knew the meaning of neither.

As the sun went into the horizon and dusk arrived, the same bird that had visited me earlier returned with a companion, also a seagull. In the golden glow of a cloudless twilight the two landed one on either side of me. They bowed their heads. I expected a prayer, perhaps a song. But instead the first bird to arrive took my middle into her beak!

Two sets of powerful wings quickly unfolded, sliced through the fresh salt air, and we rose as one into the darkening sky. Far above the sea, the white down of my feathered companions appeared like silken gold upon their slender bodies. While the first gull to visit me on the shore held me, the other bird explained God's unending love for the most insignificant, to His care for things ever present and daily seen.

Key Verse — Matthew 10:29
Are not two sparrows sold for a penny? Yet not one of them will fall to the ground apart from the will of your Father.

KEY TO A CONCLUSION: *Is it safe to assume that God knows and cares about the tiniest and most insignificant parts of His creation? Does anything happen in our lives that He isn't aware of?*

KEY TO ENCOURAGEMENT: *There is no detail God has ever overlooked. There is no concern He does not share. It is safe to say God knows us better than we know ourselves and that His love for us extends beyond what we can accomplish or become.*

On Course

Have you ever considered the golf clubs you own to be a gift from God? Because the process required to manufacture modern clubs is a long and detailed one that must be closely supervised, most golfers do not see them as a gift from their Creator.

But the truth is that God created the materials out of which your clubs were so skillfully made. Let the Lord know that the clubs He has provided for you have been a blessing.

Soon other gulls joined us from every side, forming a level flock inside the cool air, a flock that rejoiced with one heart as we flew out to sea:

As a flock we fly,

soar into dusk's last light,

to sing of God's great love,

to sing of His saving grace.

To let this driftwood know

its journey was not in vain.

Nor its love of God,

the pain it's had to bear.

For no one can wander at sea,

after thriving inside a grove,

then lay for days in darkness,

buried in the sand,

and not think about the purpose,

the meaning of all the trials.

Not question God's integrity,

the purpose of it all.

It gives this flock great pleasure,

to fly with driftwood here,

to tell this ounce of grayness,

from wandering, it is free

to become so very faithful,

a 'forever' cypress branch.

That in doing so,

all will have worked for good.

That in doing so,

all will have worked for good.

Key Verse — 1 John 1:5-7

This is the message we have heard from him and declare to you: God is light; in him there is no darkness at all. If we claim to have fellowship with him yet walk in darkness, we lie and do not live by the truth. But if we walk in the light, as he is in the light, we have fellowship with one another...

KEY TO A CONCLUSION: *Is fellowship with other Believers important to our spiritual well being? Do we need others who know Christ to encourage us in our daily walks and support our efforts to mature?*

Many Christians believe that it is not necessary to be involved in a church to grow and become all that God desires. I once knew a person who felt like the ocean was her" church" and she felt closest to Him there.

The truth is that the Bible commands us to be in fellowship with other Believers. We need to be around those who value what we do so that our faith remains strong. In our life and times, we need each other more than ever.

On Course

Why are country clubs/golf clubs/golf courses so popular across the United States? Because they allow people from all walks of life that love golf to come together and share their mutual interest. By doing so, they reinforce the value of golf in their lives. And deepen their relationship with golf and each other.

Use "God" in place of "golf" in the last three sentences and you'll see why fellowship with other Christians is essential.

Following the song the gulls were silent except for the reassuring rush of air through their wings.

Our flight above and out to sea continued as darkness enveloped the flock. Stars crept out from behind a velvety black veil. And a full moon shone brightly in the middle of the heavens, a glassy sea catching their reflection.

Moonlight splashed onto the flock and turned down and feathers silver. Of all the creatures I had met I admired birds the most. Daily they put their trust in God's winds to carry them aloft in search of food and to return them safely home.

KEY TO A CONCLUSION: *Have you ever been around a person who has known Christ for many years and knows, knows that all of God's promises are true, is more certain of it than the sun's rise at dawn?*

If you haven't, I hope you will. These mature Believers bring this verse from Hebrews home to where we live.

Because of their countless days in the sky, these gulls were as saturated with faith as I had been with water.

I had no idea where they were taking me, nor did I care to know. I understood that they trusted God as I did. And whatever happened, it would be for my good.

KEY TO A CONCLUSION: *Do you interpret this and similar verses to mean that whatever you want you will get,* *that you will receive the desires of your heart? A second interpretation is that God will place desires in your heart, and you will want to do what is in harmony with His will for your life. What do you believe to be the truth?*

On Course

Golfers and fisherman are similar in that they will often invest, without a second thought, in the latest club or gadget that will improve their chances of success. Manufacturers that supply equipment to both sportsmen cater to this tendency by coming out with new and supposedly better equipment every year.

Do we, as Christian golfers, always need the latest gear to play well and enjoy the game? Is it necessary to spend hundreds of dollars annually in an attempt to buy a better golf game? Or would we be better off taking a few lessons, reading a book, or watching an instructional video?

Before you head off to a golf shop or visit a web discount store to buy this year's version of the brand of club you play, ask God if this is His desire for you, or if the money could be better spent in some other — perhaps church related — way.

I'm not telling you to pack your bags for a guilt trip. Just stop and ask God in prayer what He wants. I did so and got a surprising answer — no.

As we soared into the night the flock let me know that they felt the pain, uncertainty and fear that I experienced on my odyssey, but could not admit. I came to realize that the flock knew about my love for Christ and my deep trust in Him. But that I once had grave doubts about the purpose of the separation, though the elders had explained the reason for it the very morning after it occurred.

Key Verse — John 14:26

All this I have spoken while still with you. But the Counselor, the Holy Spirit, whom the Father will send in my name, will teach you all things and remind you of everything I have said to you.

KEY TO ENCOURAGEMENT: *We all need people in our lives to share our concerns and trials with, someone that knows what we're feeling without having to ask. But Christ went a step further in leaving us the Holy Spirit as Comforter and Counselor. He gave us someone to rely on that is always there to encourage and guide us.*

On Course

Unless I missed the part in the Bible where it says that the Holy Spirit deserts us when we step on the golf course, He is with us there as well. And He is there in the same capacity as He is in the other parts of our lives.

Remember! Masters champion Bernhard Langer prays on the golf course. You can too. And it doesn't always have to be about golf!

Dawn came and I was still in flight with the birds. As the cool winds of morning poured over me I noticed that the gulls were flying above and below me rather than as a level group. Instead of encouraging me, they strained, fixing their gaze straight ahead, as would a mountain lion stalking its prey.

> **Key Verse — Hebrews 12:2**
> Let us fix our eyes on Jesus, the author and perfecter of our faith…

> **Key Verse — Philippians 4:13-14**
> But one thing I do: Forgetting what is behind and straining toward the goal that is ahead. I press on toward the goal to win the prize for which God has called me heavenward in Christ Jesus.

On Course

If you have followed the PGA and LPGA Tours on television over the last 10 to 30 years, you know that there are several players out there that get a look in their eyes, a confident stare that burns a hole through the competition. Their eyes are on the prize-winning trophy they seek with such intensity that they believe there is no way they will be denied.

Raymond Floyd was famous for this during his days on the regular tour and still is on the Senior Tour. Jack Nicklaus and Arnold Palmer seemed to have the ability to glare at a golf ball and will it into the hole. That was their goal and they accomplished it so many times that they are now considered among the best to ever play the game.

What about those of us who carry Christ along with our clubs? What are our goals when we play 18 holes? Christians are no different than other golfers — we want to shoot the best score we can and have fun doing it with friends. But the real challenge of golf for the Christian is being a good witness to those around us when shots go astray. Our real characters emerge when we hit a bad shot and must react to it. That is, of course, because the results of a good swing are pretty easy to take.

Ever heard the old saying, "If you want to know what someone is really like, play golf with him/her"?

We should be like Christ.

Below a group of clouds, bronzed by the sun, land appeared — a shoreline with tall, brown roughhewn cliffs. As the gap between my flock and the bluffs narrowed I saw birds coming and going and heard the distant cries of joy. These were the sounds of families being born.

As the last mile of open sea passed beneath us, a lone gull approached our flock from the cliffs with irregular, labored wing beats. Flying over and past us in a blur, the seabird turned sharply behind and caught up with the flock. She pulled even with the gull that held me in its beak, her whole body straining to keep up.

I looked into her dark brown eyes and saw a heart filled with compassion and a strong abiding love for God. He had given her wings to soar above the water and land, both providing for her and her offspring's every need.

We were nearly upon the terraced cliffs and I could see hundreds of birds nesting there. The weary gull that had joined us turned her head and peered straight into my spirit. Her eyes grew misty; tears formed and were pulled from her face by the wind. I was sure her tears were caused by sorrow.

CYPRESS TREE ODYSSEY

A sudden realization hit me. It was as if I'd been slammed hard against a sea stone by a roaring wave. This bird, the one who wept, was the same bird that had pulled me from the cypress grove. The gull, frail and old told me of its young. That the many she had raised had grown strong and flew free above the coastal waters, making families of their own on cliffs and in marshes far and wide.

I learned that she had prayed unfailingly for me since our parting.

Her tears were not filled with sorrow but with joy and thanksgiving because I had turned every last fiber of my wood and will over to God.

Key Verse — 1 Thessalonians 5:16-18
Be joyful always; pray continually; give thanks in all circumstances, for this is God's will for you in Christ Jesus.

KEY OF ENCOURAGEMENT: What is the most encouraging thing we can say to another Believer in the midst of conflict or stress (besides letting him or her know you love them)? "I'll be praying for you" or "I've been praying for you every day."

On Course

During my competitive days on my college golf team we played numerous matches against local rivals. Since many holes had adjoining fairways the members of our team often got a chance to talk to each other and find out how our individual matches were going.

If my team mate or myself were struggling we'd often encourage each other by saying, "Come on, suck it up. I'm pulling for you. We can beat these guys!"

I always came away from such "updates" with my spirits lifted and an increased desire to do my best.

The fact that someone is committing to or has committed to pray for you should be an even greater encouragement, whether it has to do with golf or not.

Still I wondered why the gull had come to greet me. Why she had labored so hard to reach me over the sea. Before peeling off and dropping away her eyes declared that I was going home!

Home? I thought deep inside myself. How could I possibly grow and again be part of the grove?

The flock proclaimed that I would come to be even more, and added,

More than you thought possible,

as animals enjoyed your shade.

More than you thought possible,

when in the riptide's grasp.

More than you thought possible,

when battered by the rock.

More than you thought possible,

when you reached the shore.

Though the words were as reassuring as those from the elders just before the lightning hit me I did not understand them. But there was no need to question what I had heard. I had learned that God reveals His wisdom not to those creatures most anxious to hear it, but to those with the patience to wait and listen.

Key Verse — Proverbs 2:1-5
My son, if you accept my words and store up my commands within you, turning your ear to wisdom and applying your heart to understanding, and call out for insight and cry aloud for understanding, and if you look for it as for silver and search for it as for hidden treasure, then you will understand the fear of the Lord and find the knowledge of God.

KEY TO A CONCLUSION: *In order to find wisdom we have to seek it. In order to find hidden treasure we have to search for it. Does finding wisdom take time? Does patience play a role?*

If you've ever watched the Discovery Channel as they have chronicled an adventurer's search for a sunken treasure ship, you know it takes time and lots of effort. And the expedition may come upon dozens of dead ends. The hunter has to be determined to keep looking even when he wants to give up. And he must be willing to listen to the council of others who have tried to find the same ship.

Remember! God will give us wisdom if we ask and believe. See John 14:14.

On Course

For those taking up the game today the chance to gain knowledge about the game comes in many forms: books, gadgets, video tapes, The Golf Channel, PGA professionals, golf schools, etc.

Notice I didn't say wisdom, because wisdom is the application of knowledge. You may know the mechanics that will cause the ball to draw or fade. But until you can make these shots happen by applying the techniques to your own swing, you don't have wisdom.

The same is true in spiritual terms. You may know that God loves you, that He has the strength to see you through any trial. But until you actually weather a storm — on the course or off — with God's help, it's only head knowledge, not wisdom.

That's why talking with more mature believers and more mature golfers can be very helpful. You can learn how God gave them the strength to endure their trials and the wisdom, often in hindsight, to understand what the Lord was doing in their lives. You can then apply that knowledge to your own.

The flock bathed me in words of inspiration and faith as the cliffs loomed ahead. We were closing in on the bluffs where I had once thought I would find my final resting — place, my sense of purpose.

KEY TO A CONCLUSION: *Have you ever looked back at a time years ago when you thought you knew what God was doing in your life and why, and in retrospect nearly laugh at those tattered old conclusions? If you've ever thought you knew what God was up to and have been wrong, you can relate.*

Just within the context of this allegory it seems absurd that our symbolic pilgrim thought that its odyssey would end when it became part of a sea gull's nest. That's because God had more journeying and far more purposes in mind than the pilgrim had for itself; a journey that was necessary so that it could be shaped further into the character of Christ.

Isn't that usually the case for us as Christians? Do we often want to take a shorter road to being more like Christ than God requires?

Over and inland a short distance beyond the colony of nests, I was released from the gull's beak as abruptly as I had slipped from it years ago. I tumbled toward earth again. But I felt no panic as my world went blurry and dizzy.

A Grateful Heart

Thank God for the measure of peace you can feel in the midst of trials because you know Him personally.

PART 10

Making Sense of the
Trials & Tests

PART TEN
Making Sense of the Trials & Tests

Caught by a field of wild meadow grass, I found myself surrounded by succulent green glades. The fresh scent of life caressing me was as wonderful as the raindrops I had tasted during my first spring above the soil.

This grass, this ground held a permanence that filled me with peace. The grass knew of my pleasure and gave this to me.

You have traveled far

to lie upon my meadow.

I know that you must wonder,

if you will wander once again.

What His nature says I tell you,

your wandering is nearly over,

that you will be planted,

inside God's Home for Man.

Though excited by the meadow's promise, if my wanderings had taught me anything, it was that growth of any kind takes time, and permanence even longer.

On Course

No one becomes great at the game of golf over night. Neither does a Believer "arrive" after knowing Christ for a day. In fact, it has been said that when you put a club in a child's hands and tell him to hit a golf ball, every natural instinct he has is wrong.

Instead of a slow, rhythmic swing that catches the ball crisply and sends it darting into the air, a short chopping action — akin to killing a snake — takes place. And the ball may not feel the sting of the club head even after several attempts.

No, learning just the fundamentals of the sport is challenging enough. Then you can add the artful science of learning to "work the ball" and all the subtleties of the short game. Whew! It's a wonder anyone comes close to mastering the sport!

The odyssey begins when the first golf ball is struck.

Handing a Bible to a person that isn't a Christian and asking him or her to live a life pleasing to God is similar. All the things that come naturally simply won't work. A person has to read The Book and get to know the God that loves him/her.

And the journey begins when Christ is accepted as Savior.

A Grateful Heart

Thank God that you accepted Him and are being made more into the likeness of Christ as each day passes.

If you haven't started the journey, find a good church and ask what you need to do to know Christ as your personal Savior.

Spring was once my favorite season, but now its arrival became another test of patience and faith.

KEY TO A CONCLUSION: *Have you ever felt that God keeps bringing the same or similar trials into your life? What do you think He is trying to teach you?*

When the fragrant spring rains came, the dormant grass beneath me turned green and the meadow vowed that I would be planted again. The promise grew more hollow than a fallen rotting tree as the years slipped by and I remained in the meadow.

Why was God taking so long to fulfill His promise?

KEY TO A CONCLUSION: *Do Christians who have spent years in the faith still ask God, "Why don't you answer me? Where are you?" Of course! In our humanness we still want answers to our crises right away — despite knowing that God may be on a different timetable than we are.*

It helps to read scripture such as Proverbs 3:5-6. We need to be reminded that God is directing our paths.

I preferred lying in the meadow to being buried in the sand. At least I could see the sky, feel the wind, and appreciate the refreshing showers that came my way.

But with each downpour my dry wood drank up the moisture, and when the sun came back out it pulled it from me just as fast.

A crack crept down the center of me just past the middle point of my length, widening with time. Though the fissure did not cause me pain, I wondered why I had to change still more. The only answer was that God's purposes would be served. I knew that to be true of even the smallest event now.

KEY TO ENCOURAGEMENT: *Just a reminder that you "can do anything through Christ who strengthens you"(Philippians 4:13). And that, "All things work for good" in your life (Romans 8:28). That means every detail, not just the big stuff.*

On Course

Does everything that happens on the golf course work for your good, even when you four putt or shoot your worst score? As was noted earlier, there is no reason to believe that golf courses are exempt from biblical principles.

But you may have to reach heaven and ask the Lord why you played the way you did on specific occasions.

The grass beyond me rustled one winter day. The grass itself, silent beneath a sky quilted in blue and white, said nothing, merely reacting to whatever was causing it to move, probably a familiar creature I had seen many times in my grove.

Whatever was coming my way knew of songs and words, but not in the usual way that God's creations related to one another. This was a language that I understood though I had never heard it before. Over the rustling blades as deep as a sea lion's growl came, "When trials like sea billows roll. Whatever my lot, thou hast taught me to say, 'It is well, it is well with my soul.'"

I was startled when the thing that cut through the grass turned out to be what the starfish had described. It was a man with two long legs, kind blue eyes, and a curious face without fur — except for small pieces over each eye that looked like caterpillars. The top of his head was covered with hair that was a mixture of gray and white. Somehow it grew around his ears without touching them.

The human's hands and arms were brown, as was the skin on this neck and wrinkled face. A curious black covering cloaked the rest of the man's body and extended to the end of his bottom limbs. Instead of paws or hooves, this creature had two oblong feet. Each foot was one piece, also black and very long and shiny. Only the skin of a dolphin matched the sheen they possessed.

His hands, attached to thick arms and broad shoulders, were warm and tender. I felt this tenderness as he bent down, grasped me, looked me over carefully and said, "Smooth yet rough; weathered but wise; having endured yet been perfected; having stood the test but remained faithful…perfect. It's perfect!"

Key Verse: Hebrews 10:14
…because by one sacrifice he made perfect forever those who are being made holy.

A Grateful Heart
Praise God for all that He accomplished through His Son's sacrifice on the cross: saving us from our sin, making us perfect in God's eyes, providing us with an eternal home, etc.

I went with him the rest of that day and, as shadows crept over the land, I was carried up a small hill to a tiny shelter. It was dark brown on each of its sides and had an opening tall enough for a man to pass through.

Just inside the opening, in the dim light of dusk, was row after row of flat, stout trees. In my wanderings, I had never come across a tree that grew as these did. Only as high as a newborn fawn, they were flat on top, devoid of branches and supported one trunk on each end. There were no roots growing out of any of the trunks and the ground they grew from was made of crimson fur.

The bark of each tree had been stripped away, and they looked as if they had been covered with seawater that refused to dry. The water's clear gloss revealed a brown grain deeper and darker than any cliff.

Beyond the evenly spaced rows, at the other end of the place, was another tree stripped bare of its bark and supported by one big trunk? The trunk was twice as high as the trees in the rows, badger brown, had a flat square top and was half as long. It was set apart from the rows and centered.

More baffling than the trees were the sides and ends of the structure and the part that hid the sky. Somehow deprived of its bark, the trees grew flat and long to cover these areas. Rain or seawater drenched this brown wood too, and its grain matched those that grew from the colored, fuzzy soil.

Just beyond the large tree that was set apart was the far end of the place. There the naked wood had grown in such a way as to create a hole with four edges of equal length; a large opening that was centered above the tallest tree. It was as if a wave had been frozen and gently placed into the wood, allowing a clear view of the outside world.

In the gathering gloom, the man produced a slender piece of golden metal from his covering that was about half my length and my same width. He slid the center of it slowly and gently into the fracture nature had opened in me.

He planted my jagged end into a hole in the center of the square on top of the largest tree.

I fit so snugly, so perfectly into it, that I was certain that this was the place I had been prepared for. I could not take credit for this fact, but could only rejoice that God had allowed me to find it at all.

Key Verse — 1 Peter 1:8-9
Though you have not seen him, you love him; and even though you do not see him now, you believe in him and are filled with an inexpressible and glorious joy, and are receiving the goal of your faith…

KEY TO ENCOURAGEMENT: *Verse 9 above concludes by saying, "the salvation of your souls." Certainly that is the goal of coming to faith in Christ. And one thing we can always find encouragement in — no matter how tough things get in this life — is that we will have a home in heaven that we are only now being prepared for.*

And it's my guess that no amount of earthly rejoicing will match the joy we will feel when we arrive at our final, eternal resting-place.

On Course

"Old golfers never die, they just retire to the 19th hole." There's some truth to that old saying. Just as we never truly "arrive" spiritually while we live out our days here on earth, we as golfers never really "arrive" either.

Most of us have moments when we, at our particular skill level, get "into the zone" and play way above our usual ability. But that is the closest we'll get to perfection. Of course, professionals like Tiger Woods function on a far higher level. But even he will never master golf, though he appears to get closer every time he plays.

For golfers then, there is a no place to arrive except the 19th hole, where the triumphs and foibles of the round just played are discussed — and sometimes bets are even paid!

The man with the silver hair knelt before the tree at the front of this Home for Man. And, with hands clasped and head bowed said softly and reverently, "Lord this driftwood and gold make the perfect cross. The gold reflects the pureness of your love, the wood your sacrifice. It was you who suffered the indignity of the cross so that a humble chaplain like me could find salvation.

"Accept my gift upon this altar. Take it with love from a humble servant. In Christ's precious name. Amen."

Slowly and reverently, the human left.

Planted in the middle of the altar, I looked out of the frozen wave to the crimson twilight mirrored on a tranquil sea. Silhouetted there in black against a sky glowing red, were trees that had huge trunks and large twisted limbs with luscious leaves.

All of my doubts about my wanderings, the trail of whys I'd left behind on every inch of my journey but shared with no one, evaporated like fog in the noonday sun. As the cypress limb that knew nothing but abundant life, being ripped away from what I was certain I was to become was traumatic and absurd.

Having survived it all because of God's grace, strength and mercy had given me a sense of direction, a purpose that had brought me to a place of worship and faith that I could never have imagined when my bark was still red.

Key Verse — Psalm 138:2
I will bow down toward your holy temple and will praise your name for your love and faithfulness, for you have exalted above all things your name and your word.

A Grateful Heart

When God shows you his faithfulness be grateful and remember how He did it. As important as praising Him for His ever-present hand in your life is, be sure to recall often what He did on the cross to show you the depth of His love — especially when life off and on the golf course becomes a struggle.

Only God, in His infinite wisdom, could have orchestrated all of the events that prepared me for and brought me here.

Growing, flying and floating, in hindsight, added to my love of God and thrilled every fiber, every dry grain of my wood that still remained. Great joy was added to the thrill when I realized that the trees that stood so eloquently against the sky were the seven cypress trees I had grown amongst. They still lived, as did the animals that, inside of His nature, had passed on life in my absence.

By some God-sent means, the animals and the cypresses must have known of my journey's end, as it was this song that reached my heart, causing the golden bar I held to glow and fill the home, the chapel by the sea with His pure light.

All beside the sea,

who call this coastline home,

know about your travels

your journey in sky and sea.

But now the wandering's over,

your odyssey is done.

And because of the separation,

you symbolize the Christ

who knew your every care

before it came to pass;

who knew you would be His,

after a difficult time.

So within His home,

praise Him in His church.

Know you are as dear to Him

as any cypress that ever stood!

Know you are as dear to Him,

as any cypress that ever stood!

I would do as they had said. And I knew, because of what Christ sacrificed for me, that nothing on earth could separate me from His love.

I was His forever.

Key Verse — Romans 8:38

For I am convinced that neither death nor life, neither angels nor demons, neither the present nor the future, nor any powers, neither height nor depth, nor anything else in all creation, will be able to separate us from the love of God that is in Christ Jesus our Lord.

Key Verse — Romans 2:7

To those who by persistence in doing good seek glory, honor and immortality, he will give eternal life.

~The End~

TAKE YOUR GAME TO THE NEXT LEVEL

Visit **www.YourOdyssey.net**, the official site of CYPRESS TREE ODYSSEY for a **FREE**, downloadable personal study guide with questions, thought provoking statements and more scripture for devotions and reflection.

Read further comments about the book from the author, and communicate with him via email through the web site about how God has used the book in your life.

So go to **www.YourOdyssey.net** and get your FREE Study Guide TODAY!

ABOUT TODD R. DUFEK

The author was born into a large Christian family in a small town in Wisconsin in the late 1950's, moving to another rural town in Arizona when he was 11-years-old. Todd spent most of his adolescence practicing and playing golf on local courses. That is, when he wasn't attending high school and working side by side with his dad in the family shoe business.

Todd played on his high school golf team for four years, his team winning the state championship twice. He attended Grand Canyon University in Phoenix, Arizona where he played on a golf scholarship, earned a

B.A. degree in Behavioral Sciences, and was named to the NAIA Academic All-American Golf Team.

He went straight to graduate school at Arizona State University and received a Masters degree in Social Work in 1982, specializing in Family and Child Welfare. Between Todd's undergraduate work and Masters Degree he spent more than half a decade working toward his goal of becoming a counselor and making a real difference in the lives of families and children.

In 1986 the world as Todd knew it collapsed. He had to call social work quits and within months his father, whom Todd admired in so many ways, died suddenly and without warning. In fact, he was the first of five children to receive the call no one wants to get from a tearful mother; "Todd, your father just died of a heart attack…" There would be no good byes.

A few months after these events, Todd found himself back at his mother's home doing much needed repairs on the house. Despite being a Christian for most of his life and thoroughly convinced that everything happens for a reason, Todd had a difficult time believing it. He had to force himself to trust the God he'd always had faith in. After all, the profession he'd studied and trained so hard for was gone…and he would never see his father again.

In the midst of his hurt and loss, Todd was forced to ask himself some hard questions: What purpose could such grief, having to endure two devastating losses at one time possibly serve? Where was the God that promised he'd never leave me? He took these questions before the Father, along with his anger, grief and despair and filled notebooks with prose that turned to poetry and an allegory.

Even before these events occurred, God had orchestrated a miracle: allowing Todd to attend a writer's conference in the Northwest that cost nearly $1,000 when he was living paycheck to paycheck as a clinical social worker. Long after these events he took a writing correspondence course that took two years to complete, but taught him the basics of the craft.

Todd had obediently walked through the literary doors that God had opened and worked hard to hone a gift he never knew he had. That conference and surviving those watershed events left Todd with a love of writing and the desire to publish a book that honored God and shared the gospel. And provided Believers and non-believers with a reason to both deepen their faith and find it, respectively.

What became abundantly clear to Todd was that God had been with him on every step of his journey, and that the trials and tests he experienced were necessary and purposeful after all. In short, his odyssey resulted in the book you hold in your hands today.

Todd resides in Phoenix, Arizona with his wife and daughter and attends a non-denominational church.

Printed in the United States
92173LV00001B